GOTTA GET SIGNED

HOW TO BECOME A HIP-HOP PRODUCER

BY MULTI-PLATINUM PRODUCER
SAHPREEM A. KING

SCHIRMER
TRADE
BOOKS

A Part of **The Music Sales Group**
New York/London/Paris/Sydney/Copenhagen/Berlin/Tokyo/Madrid

Schirmer Trade Books
A Division of Music Sales Corporation, New York

Exclusive Distributors:
Music Sales Corporation
257 Park Avenue South, New York, NY 10010 USA
Music Sales Limited
8/9 Frith Street, London W1D 3JB England
Music Sales Pty. Limited
120 Rothschild Street, Rosebery, Sydney, NSW 2018, Australia

Order No. SCH 10154
International Standard Book Number: 0.8256.7315.1

Cover Design: Josh Labouve

Printed in the United States of America

Library of Congress Cataloging-in-Publication Data

King, Sahpreem A., 1970-
  Gotta get signed : how to become a hip-hop producer / Sahpreem A. King.
    p. cm.
  ISBN 0-8256-7315-1 (pbk. : alk. paper)
  1. Sound recording industry—Vocational guidance—United States. I. Title.
ML3790.K465 2004
782.421649'068—dc22
                              2004014310

CONTENTS

Dedication

This book is dedicated to my wife, Tori A. Lovett-King,
and my children, Aren J. King, Christine A. King, and Khalil N.
King, for all of their love and support throughout my musical career.
Also, I would like to make a special dedication to the memory of
Barry Yearwood, who was an excellent manager, mentor, and friend.
Thank you for helping launch my professional career.

Acknowledgements

GOD, Mom and Dad, My Brothers, Panda, Tony, Chrissy, and Killian, My Sister Brooke R. Williams, the King Family, the Lovett Family, the Gardner Family, Audrey Cain (Combat Typist) thanks for helping me type up the book, Charlie Company 841st Engineer Battalion—"Operation Enduring Freedom," Steve Toro, Ray George, Cess and Gina Brooks, DJ Laz, Angela Beasley, Dennis "Denone" Bertty, Chad "Kaleber" Mohammed, DJ Vic Mesa, Anthony "Vitaman" St. Amand, Bert St. Amand, Joi Roberts-Wyche, Andrea "Dray" Hicks, Pablo Casals, Mike Hernandez Sr.(RIP), Mike "Mikey Gunz" Hernandez Jr., Eddie "Goalfingaz" Berkeley, Anthony "Poetic" Berkeley (RIP), Larry Williams, KRS-One, Derrick Green, Robin David, Tamara Wallace, Desmond Lowe, Marissa Stapleton, Peter "Nipsey Hustle" Reznicek, Raheem, Robert Wright, Kenny Ortiz, Sam Ash Music, Rich Bartell, Paul "the King" Delaney, Guido Osorio, Larry Dermer, SWV, Ray and Sean Brown, Emilo Estefan, Pandisc Music, Bo Crane, Jamie Graf, James Holland, Marco Ruffalo, Sony Latino, Ivy Queen, Mase (De La Soul), Milo (LONS), Big Daddy Kane, Bob Vandermark, Vanessa Rodriguez (ASCAP Miami), Ian Burke (ASCAP ATL), Wyclef Jean, Keith Murray, Eric Sermon, Mark Berto, Parrish Smith, Rakim, King Sun, Cooly Live, Dean "Gudtymes" Gibson, Tamara Johnson, RUN-DMC, Jam Master Jay (RIP), Studio Center, Mirror Image Studios, Crescent Moon Studios, RCA BMG, Universal Latino, The Kumbia Kings, Grandmaster Flash, Levant Marcus, Cruz Martinez, Lorna Owens, Shauna Solomon, Erin Forrest, Crazy Legs, the Rock Steady Crew, De La Soul, Pablo Casals, Danny "Sadam" Iglesia, Eddie Morreau, Christie D. Akins, Eric Gutherie, the Magnum Force M.C.s, Jermaine Dupri, Dallas Austin, Darryl Cochran, Anthony Cochran, Troy Brown, Ulysses "MONK" Maceo, George Clinton, Terrence Clayton, Niya Johnson, Daphne Gutierrez, SFC Luz Ortiz, Maurice Redman, Sir Jinx, Just-Ice, LL. Cool J, Freddie Foxx, DJ Khalid, P.M. Skillz, Larceny, Darryl "CHILL" Mitchell, Anthony Holmes (RIP), Robert Holmes, Shannon and Shawana Stapleton, Edward "Nard" Thomas, Matthew "DMX" Desrameux, Walter "Clyde" Orange, Simone Hylton, Sergio Rivera thanks for the Artwork, Natali Roberts thanks for the photos on the book, Paul "Dr. Paul" Hamilton, SFC Randy Thompson and SSG O'Neal Murray for always having my back, Russ from the Bay Meadows Kinko's in Jacksonville, Austin Reed, Brother Tony Mohammad Urban America Magazine, DJ Suicide, Supa Cindy WEDR 99 JAMZ, Fab 5 Freddy, Afrika and Mike G(Jungle Brothers), Jammin' Johnny Caride, Trina, Slip-n-Slide Records, Trick Daddy, Cacno Unsigned Artist Magazine, Pitbull, Garth "Sirgio" Redwood, Mic Check, Kirk Harding, Shakira Wint, Sherry McCall, Keva Hargrove, Nomadz Films, Shauna Dazzle, David Rowe, the Aficionados, Monique Glinton, Tony Galloway, Galfrie "Toppa" Balgrove, Fernando Vega Top of the World Entertainment,Pinnacle, Rox, Che'Fu, Ivy Queen, J. Bishop, The Roof, Liquinatti Family Entertainment, Slank-Ox, Noah Picasso, Third Synopsis, Rosadela Arenas, Astrid Arizmendi, Karl Avanzini, Neipy Sayans, Connecticut School of Broadcasting Staff and Students Class of 2004, Angie Lopez, Chris Hudspeth, Elmo Lugo, Marc Eisenberg, Craig Spitz, Nick Satterfield, Mark Morgan, Anthony Decesare, Adrian Baccaus, Michael D'Imperio, Isis Torres, David Weathers, Yami Gomes, Somy Ali, Leana Tomilson, Amy Oliver, Mark Turner, Miriam Gonzalez(Miss March 2001), Samantha Williams, Scott Richards, Danny Doyle, Mujaida Khan,103.5 the BEAT, Nick V, Eric V, J-Love, Prince Markie D, Special thanks to Andrea Rotondo for seeing my potential. A extra special thanks to Nathan McCall Author of the book "Makes Me Wanna Holler", your book inspired me to become a writer, thanks Man.

About the Author

Miami has developed quite the reputation for booty-bass music, strip clubs, and the infamous South Beach club scene. Veteran producer Sahpreem King is no stranger to any of these elements, which make Miami the music industry's next hot spot.

Producing tracks for artists such as SWV, Wyclef, Beenie Man, and Eric Bene't, along with the Latin flavors laid down for artists such as DJ Laz, Paulina Rubio, Ivy Queen, Tono Rosario and Fat Joe, and A.B. Quintanilla y Los Kumbia Kings, has not only elevated his productions to R.I.A.A. multi-platinum status, but also earned his music a Number One position on Billboard's Latin 50.

Sahpreem has been in the business for ten years as a DJ, programmer, and remixer. He is the sole owner and operator of the Sewer Ratz Records moniker. This beat specialist has taken the art of remixing to such extreme levels that in many cases his remixes have replaced the original versions of songs on many of the artists' albums he has produced.

In this highly competitive business of music, Sahpreem has managed to scratch and gnaw his way to the top of the heap. Defying the odds of longevity in the music business, Sahpreem King and Sewer Ratz Records have once again proven that even in a market undergoing growth, a combination of talent and good business sense can still go a long way.

Production Discography

A.B. Quintanilla Y Los Kumbia Kings
In the Zone, Need Your Love,
Break Me Off
EMI Latin

Beenie Man
Foundation Remix
V.P. Records

Booty Girlz
Booty Girlz Album
Pandisc Music Corp.

DJ Laz
Ki Ki Rimbu, Negra Chula Remix
Pandisc Music Corp.

DJ Sahpreem Featuring Rob Wright
My Girlfriend's Girlfriend
Pandisc Music Corp.

DJ Twitch
Jump On It
Pandisc Music Corp.

DJ Vic
All Out of Love
Pandisc Music Corp.

Eric Bene't
Why You Follow Me Latin Mix
Warner Brothers

Halusanation
Celebrate, Bounce
Limp-A-Lot Records

Ivy Queen Featuring Wyclef Jean
In the Zone Remix
Sony Latino

Latin Mix USA 2
Sony Latino

Lavaska
Messed It Up
Ya Mon/Universal

Miami Sound Machine
Start It Up
Crescent Moon/Sony Music

Outside Link
Outside Link
Dorado Records

P.M.
Chinese Arithmetic 99", Poly'n
Perpetual Nod Recordings

Paulina Rubio
Y Yo Sigo Aqui Tropical Mix
Universal Latino

Real Latin Mix 2002
Prisoner of Dance Recordings

SWV
Blak Pudd'n

Right Here Remix (Single)
Sahpreem's Funk Rap Show Mix
RCA Records

Thalia
Amor La Mexicana Remix
Sony Music

Tono Rosario Featuring Fat Joe
Sueltame Remix
WEA Latino

Viva Latino
Sony Music

PREFACE

I have designed this very simple guide to arm new producers with basic knowledge that every hip-hop producer should have when they first enter the game. I have chosen to write it in its most primitive form, in order to capture some of the energy and emotions I have experienced in this business of hip-hop music. If some of the language offends you, or if you don't understand the lingo, then this may not be the book for you.

INTRODUCTION

It seems that nowadays everybody and their mama's got a record label. Every time you look at a magazine, see a video, listen to the radio, or pass an SUV or minivan on twenties, somebody is bumping some unknown artist from the hood, and repping a new label. Some disillusioned individual or ex-drug dealer with hopes of becoming the next Cash Money dynasty is tossing t-shirts out of a van or talking shit at an open mic night on how they've got the hottest new artist since the late Biggie. I ain't trying to hate, 'cause anything is possible, but the truth is, dawg, the cards are stacked against you.

I have been in the hip-hop game for a long-ass time; not since its very birth, but definitely from its infancy stage. My personal journey began like so many others before me, as a quest for props and neighborhood recognition. Back in the ol' skool, hip-hop culture epitomized black manhood in the ghetto. You were known in your hood by the skillz you possessed and how well you could flex them. For example, back in the 'hood, niggahs were judged by how well you could B-boy, how nice you were with the hands, how you rocked your gear, or how well you threw up your tag, and shit like that. In my neighborhood you were praised like a king if you had verbal prowess, whether it was with spitting game to the females, or rocking the M-I-C. Man, I am dead-ass serious, the GOD Rakim was a legend in my neighborhood, long before he was ever on wax. Just out of rhyming at backyard parties and mix tapes, Rakim earned the praise of a king.

Fo' shizzle, back in the early '80s, every ghetto black male, including myself, wanted to be down with hip-hop, and all for sheer love of the game. It's funny (in a tragic sense) how shit has all changed, for the game and for myself. Back in the day, nobody was getting paid like they are now, and nobody really cared. It was all for sport and neighborhood recognition. Now, all niggahs are hollering 'bout is bling bling, money and bitches. Where did we lose focus? As a direct result of this, over the years hip-hop and I have formed a love-hate relationship, sort of like an Ike and Tina Turner marriage on steroids.

I got in the game out of love for the mic; I stayed in the game out of love for the money; and I left the game out of respect for the culture. Don't get that shit twisted, son; I ain't no burnt-out wannabe-never-was niggah who couldn't take the pressure, not by any means. I am more like a retired Captain in the Hip-Hop Army (we all know Master P is the General). And like any eager recruit, I rose swiftly through the ranks, first, as a B-boy (breaker); then as a rapper; then a DJ, artist, promoter, writer, multi-platinum producer, engineer and studio owner; and finally business manager and independent label CEO. I have been in videos, been a radio DJ, been on tour (as a rapper, dancer, and DJ), dated famous female artists, and befriended many of music's most famous and infamous characters.

In total, I have touched, tasted, and seen many things in this world. If I had listened to my sixth-grade music teacher, who said I had "zero musical talent and should stick to sports," I probably would have not experienced any of these things at all. Shit, if I had a nickel for all the times so-called friends and family members said I should "give up that music shit, and get a job," I would be richer than Donald Trump. In my opinion, I have had a successful run. Others may beg to differ, but a smart man never measures his accomplishments by another man's ruler.

Though the game has been a roller coaster ride for me, all rides must come to an end. There have been times when I was homeless and times that I was hopeless. There have been times that the money was flowing like water and times when the well was dry. There were times when I felt like I was "King of Niggah Mountain" Nate McCall, and times I felt like a niggah getting raped in jail with *no Vaseline*. Though this is my story, I hope that you can find some of this shit I'm spitting to be useful in your own journey, even if you do the opposite of what I have done. Remember that something good can always come out of a fucked-up situation, and nothing in this game of life is free: Everything costs somebody somewhere, somehow, something at some time. Choose your battles wisely and also remember: AIN'T NO RULES IN THIS GAME. Then ask yourself, would you rather get fucked by someone who tells you they're gonna fuck you and does it, or someone who lies to you about it and fucks you anyway? Remember that this is a business created by thieves and money launderers, who strongly oppose thievery, such as sampling, CD piracy, and file-sharing, except for when it benefits them. So when in Rome, act like the Romans, and always know what you're getting your ass into.

Peace,
Sahpreem King

HISTORY OF HIP-HOP MUSIC
AND THE MAINSTREAM MEDIA

Yo, it's Sprite! In 1985 the legendary forefather of rap, Kurtis Blow, set it off by becoming the first hip-hop artist to ever appear in a television commercial. The Coca Cola Company took a huge risk when they decided to use a rap star as a tool to market their soda to inner-city youth. Needless to say, their idea paid off in a major way. During this time period, America was still afraid of the hip-hop culture, so whoever was the idea man behind this marketing campaign at Sprite had huge balls and needs to be given a hip-hop lifetime achievement award. His foresight was responsible for marrying hip-hop and mainstream media.

For real, son, when I saw that commercial, I was about 15 or 16 years old, just beginning to get my feet wet in the game. Even then, I possessed enough knowledge to understand that the world of hip-hop, as I knew it, was all about to change. Sure, Run-D.M.C., rap's royal impresarios, had written catchy phrases referencing name brands in their braggadocio styles of tongue, but none of their attempts hit you in the chest like a ton of bricks the way the verses Kurtis Blow kicked on my TV screen did, that first time the commercial aired. In a tragic sense, it's funny that even though I was outwardly happy that hip-hop had broken down the corporate doors, I was inwardly saddened by the fear of its death and destruction caused by commercialism.

Here's why. American pop culture is a monster that systematically and consistently chews you up and spits you out. Yeah, I know we should all have been popping bottles of Moët, toasting the good life, but most intelligent thinkers, including myself, were in fear for our lives. Understand that when I say this I don't mean it in the literal sense of death, but in the way that a 40 oz. of Old English (if you still drink forties, you're wrong) gets stale if you sit it out too long. We're talking about shelf life, homie. See, in the grand spectrum of things, hip-hop culture is a worldwide network of communities, wherein every artist is in direct or indirect association with one another. Every rapper can contribute his career in some way to the success and talent of another rapper. Whether an artist was brought into hip-hop's inner circle by another rapper, or influenced by the talents of another rapper, the two have formed an unbreakable link. Every artist believes in the hip-hop culture and the many principles that it represents. Therefore, if hip-hop were ever to be destroyed, it would result in a catastrophic domino effect, destroying the hopes, dreams, and lifestyle of all of its cultural practitioners. Think about it; this shit is real deep. Heads base their entire purpose for breathing on hip-hop. If hip-hop dies, then we as hip-hop artists die.

Public Enemy Number One: Mainstream Media!

Before I was an author, before I was a producer, before I was a rapper or even a DJ, I was a break dancer. Go to any party, club, or backyard jam, I was there, smack dab in the middle of the floor, busting out the latest B-boy moves. Every day after school, my break dance crew and I would bust out our cardboard dance floors and practice until the streetlights came on or everybody's moms called them home for dinner. We would dance on street corners to collect enough money to buy stuff like suede Pumas, matching Adidas sweat suits, and boom boxes. On the weekends, we would gather up our loot and catch the bus downtown to the mall, so we could see the latest break dance movie that was playing. We saw everything about a hundred times or more, from "Wild Style" to "Breakin'," and the classic "Beat Street." Like true students, we watched and studied every move until those movies helped us take our skills to the next level.

Suddenly, out of nowhere, break dancing became a world phenomenon. It was like a man who had won the lotto and suddenly moved out of the hood. Break dancing was everywhere. Little middle-class suburban white kids (no offense to little middle-class suburban white kids) were on Sesame Street, break dancing with Bert and Ernie, popping and locking with Big Bird. I swear, there was a commercial for Fruity Pebbles with Fred Flintstone and Barney Rubble break dance-battling for a bowl of cereal. It had gotten way out of hand. The world had gone bananas over break dancing, and corporate America was right in the midst of it, making all of the proceeds. Once the mainstream media sank their fangs into it, they sucked it dry, just like a vampire bat.

By the late '80s the media blitz was over, and nobody had an interest in break dancing anymore. The once-crowded dance floors that had parted like the Red Sea at the mere thought of a B-boy battle were now tighter than a virgin's thighs. Cats all across the globe were tossing out their cardboard and hanging up their Adidas suits. Corporate America was killing break dancing faster then the Ebola virus was killing Africans. Hope was almost lost, but some true B-boys from up in the Bronx have kept it alive all these years by nursing it back to health in the underground hospitals wherein it was birthed. In fact, I'd like to personally thank Crazy Legs and the RSC (Rock Steady Crew) for keeping this shit real. 'Nuff respect, FAMILY.

Corporate America Goes for Round Two

Now, nearly a decade and a half later, hip-hop is once again on Corporate America's dinner plate. Throughout the years, hip-hop has dodged more than its fair share of bullets from its mortal enemies, such as C. Deloris Tucker and various other political assassins who will remain nameless. If it wasn't for brothers like Tupac (RIP) and hip-hop mogul Russell Simmons, who weren't afraid to call these media snipers from out of the shadows and expose them to the world, hip-hop would probably not be alive and flourishing today.

But wait a minute. Here in the new millennium, hip-hop's newest enemy doesn't wear a Brooks Brothers suit. It isn't a Harvard-educated attorney with a corner office and a killer view of the city. In fact, it isn't even the Indian cat on the corner, selling bootlegged copies of your CD. Hip-hop's newest enemy looks like you, dresses like you, and probably sounds like you too. The media has finally managed to flip the script on us. First it was East coast/West coast, then Tupac and Biggie (RIP), Jayz and Nas, now it's 50 Cent and Ja Rule. Nowadays niggahs are taking their beefs way further than just on wax. Ask P. Diddy about that shit. The sad part is that hating one another is just a fraction of the real problem. Ever since American media made overnight superstar millionaires out of rappers, these niggahs think that they're invincible and fail to realize that with stardom comes a lot of responsibility: Responsibilities that a lot of these cats are unable to deal with. As soon as everybody got on the bling bling shit, we were headed for destruction. All these cats seem to care about is ice, ass, and cash. Just listen to the lyrics in the songs. Hold up, dawg, don't let me forget: Everybody is a hardcore thug and gangster. Niggah, please. True gangsters don't rap; they kill. I thought NWA left all that gangster shit back in the '80s.

It's painfully obvious that the next generation of consumers could give a rat's ass about hip-hop's negative portrayal and bad-boy image. Back in 1986, when Eric B. and Rakim dropped "Eric B. for President," they completely changed the way emcees flowed on the mic. Rakim's lyrical content and style were so innovative that he unknowingly caused millions of other rappers to tighten up their game and take it back to the lab. More recently, rappers like Nas, Eminem, Ludacris, Jadakiss, and Jayz have kept niggahs on their tippy toes, trying to compete lyrically, but for the most part the buying audience doesn't give a fuck if you can flow or not. Muthafuckas don't care anymore how well you can rap; they just want a catchy hook line and a crunk-ass beat. This is the very reason you hear so much bullshit on the radio, and of course the clubs follow the same trends set by the radio, so that's how these bullshit songs go platinum. Puff Daddy said it best: "It's all about the Benjamin's baby." How many records can you sell, how fast can you drop the next record, and how many times can you talk about the same lame-ass shit on one record? Fuck lyrical integrity, fuck lyrical content; just drop an album every six months and keep it real krunk. By utilizing sources of media such as music videos and the Internet, this garbage is spoon-fed to the average hip-hop consumer on a daily basis. No-one in the industry seems to question the content of these records, unless they're not making their pockets fatter by promoting them. It used to be that only every now and then some bullshit rap record would slip through the cracks and take the industry by storm. I guess somebody was sleeping on guard duty the day they opened the floodgates to the cesspools and let out all the shitty rappers. Good marketing and lots of cash can be blamed for exposing those who should never have been exposed. Think for a second. Which is more difficult: Wrapping shit in a gold package or wrapping gold in a shit package? Don't allow your eyes to do the listening that your ears should be doing. All that glitters is certainly not gold.

In conclusion, we as a hip-hop nation have an obligation to effectively control our careers and learn to use the power of the mainstream media to our advantage. Do like Oprah Winfrey and gain enough power and prestige so that the media becomes your little bitch, ready to be pimped. I think the next time I see a millionaire rapper being interviewed and talking about all the materialistic shit he owns, while the niggah can't even put a sentence together without saying "nawmean" or "I'm saying though," I'm gonna spill my cookies all over my brand new FUBU shirt.

2

PRODUCER OR BEAT-MAKER: WHAT A PRODUCER REALLY DOES

First and foremost, I need to get this off my chest. I'm tired of all these cats claiming that they're producers when, in fact, they are only beat-makers.

- **Rule Number One:** If you have never spent at least three days locked up in a studio with no sleep and a shit load of Cuban coffee, you are probably not a producer.
- **Rule Number Two:** If you haven't worked on a snare for about two hours just to get it sounding tight, you are definitely not a producer.
- **Rule Number Three:** If you've never argued with a stubborn artist half the night over how they should sing the hook you wrote, well, dawg, you are by no means a producer.

Don't be scared; there is hope for you yet, young Jedi. Everybody had to start out somewhere, and a demo copy of Fruity Loops is as good a place as any to begin. I mean, damn, when I think back to the shit we had when I started in the '80s, I don't know whether to laugh or cry. Back in the day, equipment was very bulky and hard to come by. Not too many stores carried professional recording equipment, plus funds were mad limited.

As a matter of fact, when I was fourteen, I was in this rap group called the Magnum Force. I ain't lying, this was back when rappers had names so long that you needed a name belt and sweat jacket just to spell out your name. Fucked up as it may seem, we thought we were the shit back then. My name was the Supreme Romeo M.C. Devastator. Now try saying that three times really fast. You're liable to go into convulsions.

Anyway, back then, the most high-tech equipment we had was two turntables and a drum machine. Nowadays you can have an entire studio in your computer, and for less than the price we paid for one hour's worth of studio time. Crazy, but these days, everywhere you turn there are studios popping up. It seems as if the world has gotten Hip-Hop Hysteria or something. Though today's world seems to be hooked on hip-hop like it's crack, people still seem to overlook the fact that hip-hop is an art form and production is a craft. To be a successful producer, you must be a craftsman. As I always say, "leave no record unplayed and no beat unjacked."

Every sound can be used in some form or fashion, and armed with a Technics SL-1200 and a good sampler, the only thing that can hold you back is a lack of imagination. Sampling is the bread and butter tool of hip-hop production, and, son, you better learn to master this craft if you want to eat. Do not be afraid to experiment, manipulate sounds, and duplicate or rearrange things to suit your needs. Everybody samples, even the greats.

As a producer, you must also look at yourself as the coach of a winning team. Think of your artists as your star players and learn how to develop their talents without overwhelming their abilities. There is a thin line between pushing artists to their limits and pushing them over the edge. I had to learn that lesson the hard way. Once I was in the studio with a new female singer who was quite nervous, and unsure of her talents. We had been working on a vocal harmony for about two-and-a-half hours. The funny thing was that, every time she came from out of the vocal booth to practice the harmony, she got it right, but when she went back into the booth to commit it to tape, she would totally fuck it up. Nearing hour three, I was fried. My patience was very thin and I was utterly pissed the fuck off. I lost it, and started screaming and cussing like I was Ike Turner or something. She was so upset that she burst into tears and started trembling. Then in anger she took off her headphones and threw them at the vocal booth window smashing them into a million pieces. I knew she was mad, but I kept rubbing it in deeper and deeper until she finally ran out of the studio. Within five minutes she had called her manager and the studio owner and I was fired and asked to leave the premises. Pointless to say, I never got paid and I was banned from working at that studio ever again. I don't know what had gotten into me that night, but not knowing when to draw the line cost me a whole lot more than just my time, it cost me money and reputation.

Build a strong personal relationship with the artist, and you are almost guaranteed a successful working relationship as well. If the artist is female, attempt to build this structure without trying to get her into bed. In the long run the only person you'll be fucking is yourself (out of time and money).

Treat your artist like the fine china your mom only takes out on special occasions and holidays—they are extremely fragile. Remember, artists are creative people and emotionally driven. They are not business-minded, but as a producer you must be both creative and business-minded. Plus, a lot of the projects will be consumed by external constraints, like time and money. So don't expect them to care about your budget or schedule. Learn to roll with the punches and be flexible.

What is a Hip-Hop Producer?

A hip-hop producer is simply someone who produces hip-hop music. In essence, the producer is the person responsible for taking a song in its most basic form and turning it into a finished record. At times, as a producer, you must wear two hats. In the first instance, you have to be the creative force behind the project. In the second instance, and at the same time, you must control the business side of the project. There is also a third aspect I did not mention, which is the technical side of the project, but as a new producer you don't need to be concerned with that right now.

Although the ability to master both jobs at once is an excellent skill to have, it is more important for a hip-hop producer to be a good people person. Believe me, some of these artist are out of their damn minds and need to have their egos catered to, so sometimes you will feel like a high-priced babysitter. On the other hand, if you are bad with people, your ass is going to sink faster than the Titanic in quicksand. In short, a producer has to really know how to deal with different people and their different attitudes.

DJ-ing

Back in the day, when I was coming up, most of the time the DJ in a rap group was the producer of the group's records. For whatever reason, the DJ was not given due credit for his creative talents. Even though real heads always knew the truth, the DJs were eventually given their overdue respect, and sometimes a paycheck. By the early '90s, the dark ages when the DJ played second string to the rapper had come to an end. Hip-hop legends such as Marley Marl, Jazzy Jeff, Pete Rock, DJ Premier, and Dr. Dre were recognized as the driving creative forces behind the phat beats that blew up boom boxes and Cerwin Vega speakers throughout the ghetto. After all, the DJ is the one who controls the sound, and the producer is the one who creates the sound, so logically they go hand-in-hand. I myself was a DJ before putting on many of the other hats that I have worn along my journey to success. Mixing, scratching, and cutting up the ones and twos armed me with the ability to choose hot beats, manipulate sounds, and keep the crowd dancing all night.

Beat-Making

The art of DJ'ing is the second-most used tool in the hip-hop producer's bag of tricks. I think most will agree that the foundation of hip-hop production is the beat, and the DJ controls the beats. If the beats aren't bumping, nobody cares how nice the MC is; they all just want to kill the DJ. All you need is a fat-ass kick and a crispy snare, and you got a hit. Phat beats are what have distinguished hip-hop music from every other form of music in the world. Every hip-hop producer is on a personal quest to seek out new and innovative ways of making beats. Phat sounds and unique patterns are the lifeblood of the hip-hop producer.

I myself have spent countless hours and thousands of dollars on break-beat records, sample CDs, and drum machines, in order to find the phattest sounds. When I was coming up, there was an industry rumor about a record shop in Queens, on Jamaica Avenue. It was rumored that the Large Professor, Q-Tip, and Pete Rock used to shop there for beats. Naturally, as a fan of their production skills, I found my way to that very shop. I spent many hours in this dusty, mildew-smelling hole in the wall, digging for hidden treasures or new gems that had never been touched by any DJs' or producers' hands for the purpose of sampling. I would spend up to $100 per record, just to find a section that was tight enough to drop on a hip-hop track. Some might even say it was an obsession, but if it was, then I was a hip-hop-obsessed junkie. I would listen for hours to find a break that was unused by another producer, and quickly scoop up that record and dash back to the lab to try it out. Man, it was all about the beat. Shit, James Brown's "Funky Drummer" break is probably one of the most-used samples in hip-hop to date, but you can chop it up and throw it on a record tomorrow and it will still bang as hard as it did when Marley first used it back in the day.

It's funny how music can define your life. I can tell you exactly where I was the day I first heard Run-D.M.C's single "Sucker M.C.s." More importantly, I can tell you exactly how it made me feel. Even though I had been introduced to hip-hop a few years before that single dropped back in 1983, that moment in time had such a profound effect on me that it literally changed my life. The beat paralyzed my entire body from the very moment the DJ dropped the needle on the wax. I loved that record so much that I went out and bought it the very next day from a local record store. When I took it home, I played it at least 100 times before my mom got sick of hearing it and made me shut it off. I was so impressed by what I heard that I had to know who produced it, so I sat down and read the credits. Believe it or not, the one and only Russell Simmons produced that record. Russell had produced a disco record called "Action" around the same time and used the same beat for "Sucker MCs." That shit was nothing less than amazing, and it introduced me to the notion of sampling and using the drum machine together in the same song. Believe me, the TR 808 bass drum was so banging that I was instantly hooked, like it was dope. That jam dropped nearly twenty years ago, and today the 808 sample is still as much a part of hip-hop production as a Technics SL-1200 and the DJ.

Therefore, the concept of beat-making supports the theory that a producer is only as good as the sounds and samples he chooses to use. If you want to become a hip-hop producer, then you must amass an arsenal of sounds to manipulate. Just as important as the sampled sounds a producer uses is the equipment he uses to process and manipulate these sounds. In the '80s, heavyweight hip-hop pioneer and super-DJ Marley Marl used equipment such as the Akai MPC 60, EMU Emulator, and Ensoniq Mirage, to name just a few. In the early '90s, soul brother #1 Pete Rock freaked the hottest joints of his era using the Akai S950 and the infamous EMU SP1200, which gave him a distinctive beat signature.

These days, multi-platinum record producers and all-around rap giants, such as Timbaland and the RZA, create unique and totally abstract works of art with equipment like the Ensoniq ASR10, Novation Bass Station, Roland Groove Box, and Akai MPC 3000/2000XL. Regardless of the tool they use to create the hits, though, the one thing that they all have in common is that they manipulate samples and sounds to their advantage.

Sampling

It is no big secret that all hip-hop songs are composed of samples in some form or another. Sampling is the lifeblood of every hip-hop producer, being as much a part of hip-hop production as the electric guitar is a part of rock 'n' roll. A sample is a recorded section extracted from a sound recording, or a reproduction of a written composition, used with or without the permission of the original artist or composer.

Back in the day, a hip-hop producer was able to get away with grand larceny; in fact, I cannot name one old school hip-hop joint that didn't utilize someone else's material. It all began with cats like Kool Herc back in the late '70s, who would mix the break of two identical records back and forth on the turntables while the M.C. ripped the mic. This phenomenon became known as break-beat mixing and was the birth of hip-hop sampling. I swear, some of these cats were straight-up jacking for beats, but the innovators would spice up the breaks by adding background beats with the use of drums and scratching for effect.

Today, most music publishing and record companies have teams of trained employees who listen to hip-hop records day and night, searching every beat, break, and groove for the unauthorized usage of samples from songs their companies represent or own the rights to. Basically put, these assholes sit around all day looking for ways to fuck you over. If you really think about it, the whole thing is plain stupid. It's common knowledge that if it wasn't for sampling, hip-hop would not even exist, so why do these record company jerks wanna look up your ass with a microscope every chance they get? It's just another way of getting their fat asses richer. Sampling is the basic foundation of hip-hop music and will continue to be interwoven in all of its forms, as long as there are DJs still making people dance.

Sample clearance is the process whereby permission is obtained from the owner of a song (the person who wrote it) or a master recording (the person who recorded it) that you wish to use in your production. As for getting sampling clearance, don't worry about it right now: Leave that up to the executives at the label that hire you to produce records. Ultimately, if you didn't straight up do an M.C. Hammer and jack the entire record, there isn't too much to worry about...Unless, of course, the records sells millions of copies worldwide, then you can almost guarantee that some old, washed-up artist will arrive from out of nowhere with his hand out, looking for some of your publishing money. Shit, they ought to be paying you for dragging their asses from out of obscurity, but the world is an imperfect place.

Personally, I have had a run-in or two with the sample police, but like I told them, "I am innocent...I was just in the wrong place at the wrong time." Seriously, all jokes aside, I stole samples from two heavyweights in the industry and got off scot-free. Put it this way: One of them wanted 50 percent of my copyright ownership and publishing royalties just to entertain the thought of anyone sampling his material. Basically, by agreeing to this madman's terms, the licensing fees alone would have screwed me and the artist out of any royalties on the song. As for the other guy, he doesn't allow anyone to sample his works ever, but that guy has got a Napoleon complex, if you ask me.

Faced with a deadline, my paycheck on the line, I hired a musician to come in and overdub the samples I had originally stolen from these artists. Then I took that shit to the next level and changed the notes of the melody just enough for it to be deemed an original composition. Plus I had the nerve to turn around and copyright that shit too. If you find yourself in a similar situation, just do as I did; if it doesn't work out, just use the original sample, have the musician play over it and call it an interpolation, like everybody else does. Then all you have to do is pay a small licensing fee for usage, just like any rock band doing a cover song.

Getting in the Game

Too often, young producers ask me for advice on what they should do in order to get into the music business. I swear, MTV and BET have got these young heads fucked up in the game. They seem to think that they should wake up one day and start a record label with not even the slightest idea of how to do it. Indeed they should one day start a label, but first they must understand that a lot of planning and development goes into starting your own business. Yeah, it's true. They just might someday become the next Birdman/Cash Money Empire, but it takes time, dedication, patience, and, most of all, tons of cash.

There are some basic fundamentals you need to know about business before you dive head-first into this bottomless pool, without a life preserver. I must repeat myself again: *You need tons of cash.* You must also learn to be resourceful—extremely resourceful—and keep in mind that image is everything: You gotta fake it before you make it.

Usually, when I am faced with this kind of difficult question, my gut reaction is to tell them, "Don't waste your time, son." On the flipside, it all depends on where that individual is in his career. Check it: If you got a little name for yourself and some street credibility, then just maybe you'll have half a chance. But if you just bought your first set of turntables and a sampler, then my answer is, "Hell's the fuck no." Times are rough out there, kid—for real. I am not trying to ruin your wet dream or playa-hate on some American Idol-type shit, but I'm saying though, it's real hard to turn nothing into something, and especially overnight.

Here's what I suggest, if you are a producer and you are serious about blowing up on the hip-hop scene. Instead of trying to start your own record label and face the impossible, start your own production company instead. Think about it, dawg; you are a producer, so why not invest in yourself first before you try to go out there and invest in others? First, get up off the couch, put down the blunt, and go out and buy some basic production tools (which I will get into in Chapter 3, *Build a Lab and Create a Monster*. Second, fire your partner and you know who I'm talking about—the partner that's been holding you back all your life: Procrastination. That's right, playa, you gotta stop procrastinating. The only thing holding you back is you, or maybe the lack of Benjamin's. But before you go out and spend this month's rent money on equipment, there are a few basics concepts you need to follow:

Rule Number 1: Do Not Open a Recording Studio

Don't go out and buy a whole bunch of equipment that you are unfamiliar with or have no idea how to use. It makes no sense to buy a piece of equipment for $1,500 and only learn how to use ten percent of it. You will screw yourself out of $1,350, and for what? Maybe you'll impress some idiot with all the pretty buttons and flashing lights, but that's all. Stop tripping, son; it ain't that serious. You have to budget wisely and learn not to over-indulge or become the victim of some silver-tongued salesman at your local music store. Getting the wrong gear will definitely waste more time and more money than your budget will allow. The key to success here is to buy only the necessary tools you need to get the production workload done.

Leave all the high-tech mixing and engineer crap to a professional studio. This way you will guarantee that your product will be professionally recorded, and in the long run you will save money and time. But if you are a producer and an engineer, then ignore everything I just said. Then again, if you are a pro, why the hell are you reading my book, anyway?

Listen, dawg, all jokes aside, if you got your heart set on opening a commercial studio, and you are serious about becoming a producer, do yourself a favor and quit while you are still ahead of the game. If you don't, I can guarantee that you will spend more of your time recording other people's crap than you will spend recording your own. Then, when it's time for you to work on your own projects, you will be mentally drained and creatively exhausted. Take it from me; I have spent count-less nights recording other people's shit, in order to keep my studio afloat. I'm serious, kid—bills will have you lying to these cats just to make a dollar. When you work just to keep the lights from being shut off, your work suffers.

Rule Number 2: Do Not Work With More Artists Than You Can Handle

In fact, if you are just getting started, forget about signing any artist. Artists are like sinking ships stranded in the middle of the sea, and, believe me, you do not want to be a passenger on that boat. I am not try-ing to turn you off dealing with artists, but signing artists shouldn't be your main concern right now. First, you need to get yourself established as a producer before you try to put on your click. Get a few productions or remix credits under your belt before you try to sign any artist. In fact, the first artist you should sign to your production company should be you. You are your own best asset; you can control your own career. In the music business, this arrangement is referred to as being an artist-producer. Therefore, launching your career is your production compa-ny's main goal, not trying to spread yourself too thin.

Furthermore, artists can be real pains in the ass. Check this sce-nario: Say you sign Artist X for a 12-song demo production deal for a period of a year. You work with this artist about 40 hours on a song. That's almost 500 hours spent on this project. By your calculations, your time is worth a minimum of $25 per hour, and your songs are worth at least $1,500 per track. That works out to $12,500 for your time and $18,000 for your tracks. Suppose you record the project at your own pre-production studio at the discounted rate of $20 per hour. You mix the project at a professional recording studio at the rate of $60 per hour. Now, multiply the recording time by 250 hours and the mixing time by 250 hours, and that equals a whopping total of $5,000 for the pre-production and $15,000 for the mixing time. Add it all together and you have invested just over $50,000 in an artist who has no deal yet.

But wait, there's more. Artist X is super-talented, but is mad impa-tient and has a laundry list of problems that he or she brings to the studio every day. The biggest problem the artist has stems from not hav-ing money, which you don't have either (oh, by the way, that $50,000 we discussed before is purely hypothetical). You only kicked out the five grand from your pocket for the mixing time. Plus, you had to beg, borrow, and steal to get that money. To make matters worse, Artist X couldn't give a shit about your pockets 'cause he's got his own money problems to deal with.

Okay, one of your boy's is an intern at the BIG record label down the street and has managed to get you a sit-down with the A&R. All is well, but Artist X shows up about half an hour late, because he had a fight with one of his babies' mamas on the way to the meeting. Any hope for a deal just went up in smoke like the weed he walked in smelling of. You just lost all your props with the A&R and your boy for wasting the time of everyone at the label. Still holding on to the last shred of your dignity, you bounce with your product and wait for the next opportunity to get your shit heard.

At this point, a few weeks have gone by and Artist X has grown even more impatient. Besides, you haven't heard back from the ten other labels you sent your product to. Okay, it's Saturday night, and Artist X is holding down the bar at the local night spot. He runs into Mr. G., who is a drug dealer gone legit and who just started his own label, Dope Boy Records. After a few drinks, they get to talking, and being that Artist X is broke as fuck, he is mesmerized by the iced-out chains, champagne, and big car lifestyle that Mr. G. represents. After a brief discussion, the two strike up a deal. Mr. G. offers your artist $10,000 cash to bail out on you and to sign with Dope Boy Records. As a bonus, Mr. G. lets him drive around in his new Benz and floss in his iced-out jewels.

So, my friend, guess where that leaves you? Up a creek without a paddle. And, to add insult to injury, you just got a call from a real label offering your artist a record deal. You've been played, homie.

The moral of the story is to remember the golden rules. The man with the gold makes the rules. If you cannot afford to pay the artist, don't sign the artist. Money controls all that is around you, and this is a business controlled by money. Ultimately, you must think of this as a job. For example, your job gives you money in exchange for the work you do; in essence your job controls you, because it gives you money to live on. The same thing applies to your relationship with the artist: You got to come off the Benjamin's if you plan to get things done. Believe me, if you pay the artist, the result will be much better.

But before we get off the topic, as an up-and-coming producer, you should not be concentrating on working with any artists, but on yourself and your career success. Once again, you must establish yourself first, and the best way to accomplish this great task is to become known in the industry as a hip-hop producer who does remixes. In the beginning, you might have to assist a well-known producer or DJ on their projects or do your own remixes of popular songs for free. Sometimes, you might have to go out and find a cappella songs that are close to your production style and mix them over your tracks. By marrying the two you will be able to give the listener a good idea of your production and remixing skills, without having to listen to an empty beat or an artist they have never heard of. You never know—if it's tight and the A&R is feeling the mix, you may wind up with a remix or production deal with a label.

Also, try to meet and build relationships with as many record company A&R people as possible. Join as many music organizations as you can afford. There are also a ton of them out there whose membership won't cost you a dime. In addition, create a basic one-page biography of yourself, including your name and contact information, as well as a few paragraphs of information about yourself and your musical accomplishments. Most importantly, this package must look professional and be of good quality. It must also include your demo CD, showcasing your hottest material. First impressions are always lasting ones, and if your shit is hot, son, word of your skills will spread like a forest fire, so before you know it you will be on top of the game.

Rule Number 3: Learn to be Humble

No matter how tight you and your homies might think your beats are, it is always wise to play it cool and be as humble as possible. Check yourself. Nobody likes a producer with a big-ass ego, especially if you don't have the track record to match your big-ass head. Look, young buck, you have to pay your dues, so know your shit before you open your mouth. Nothing is a greater turnoff for a record executive than an egotistical, asshole producer who thinks his shit don't stink and acts like he knows it all. Cockiness gets you nowhere in this business; in fact, a lot of the time you'll have to downplay your talents and tiptoe around the industry people when you can, because it can make the difference between going to the bank and going home with your pride in your hand. A hip-hop producer is only as good as his last hit, and believe me you will make a whole lot of records between hits, so if you want to eat you better learn to be humble when the game calls for it.

The Producer's Job Redux—A Checklist

There are three essential phases in the record-making process: Pre-production, production, and post-production. Below is a simplified list of what makes up each process.

Pre-Production

Here are a few of the demands on a producer during pre-production. Do you have what it takes?

Songwriting

Song selection

Hiring of musicians/talent

Key/tempo selection

Demo recording

Rehearsals

Tape transfers

Sample clearance

Production

Once production begins, you'll need to handle these tasks.

Tracking of music

Vocal tracking

Overdubs

Background vocal tracking

Rough mixing

Post-Production

A producer's job is just beginning during post-production. Here's what's on tap.

Editing

Remixing

Final mix

Mastering (this should be left up to the professionals)

Dig this you big ol' pimp, by now I'm sure you have gotten the gist of what I have been pumping in your veins throughout this entire chapter? Any fool with a drum machine can make beats, but a producer doesn't just make beats, a producer makes records, and hot records get you platinum albums. So of course if you go platinum then your pockets will be laced with nothing but cheddar and stacking cheese is never a bad thing, right? It's simple math, do you want to get paid, or just pay the cost? Producer or beatmaker: Which one do you wanna be?

3

BUILD A LAB AND CREATE A MONSTER

So you wanna be a hip-hop producer huh? Well, before you get started, it may be the right time to crawl underneath your bed and pull out your old piggy bank and crack it open, or maybe you could ask Mom and Dad to lend you the use of the family credit card. Either way, it is time to go shopping for some equipment. Think about it, a cowboy wouldn't be much of a cowboy, without his six shooter, horse named Trigger, and one of those stupid ass looking ten gallon hats, right. Well, a producer wouldn't be much of a producer without the proper gear to produce music with, now would he? To be perfectly honest, when it comes to equipment there are a ton of options available and they are so similar in functions and features that they are merely separated by user preference. The choice is ultimately left up to you the consumer, but since we came this far together, its only right that I continue to pave the path to success for you.

Hip-Hop Production Tools

At a bare minimum, these are a few of the necessary pieces of equipment that an upcoming producer is going to need.

Computer

This is the brain of your entire operation. Not only can you use it to record and mix your music, it can also be used to organize your business affairs.

PC: Be sure to purchase one with at least a 500MHz Pentium 4 chip, 512MB of RAM, a 40GB hard drive, an internal modem, and a 16x CD burner. Also add 512MB of extra memory and an additional 60GB of internal 7200 RPM hard drive capable of recording and playing audio.

Mac: G4 or better, 512MB of RAM and at least a 40GB 7200RPM hard-drive capable of recording and playing audio.

PC or Mac? Which is better?

This is a debate that will last longer than the Crusades did, so there is no sane reason for me to add my two cents in. Bottom line is that they both work, so once again the choice is yours.

Soundcard

The first thing you do is to get rid of the soundcard that comes with the computer. Forget what they told you; it sucks for recording audio at a professional level. There are many manufacturers that make tight-sounding audio cards for cheap, but keep in mind that you want expandability.

Audio Program

What you are looking for is a program that offers audio recording, editing, sequencing, and mastering all in one. See list of audio programs in the resource section of the book. Also, if you ever have to load an audio program into Windows, you'll know you want something that eliminates the pain and suffering that comes from brain-wrestling with the computer.

All-In-One Units

Later on I'm going to tell you to stay away from all-in-one equipment, but here is the exception to that rule. Carillon USA (www.carillonusa.com) is a company that sells turnkey computer systems specifically designed for audio recording and production. All systems are specifically designed and configured to meet the needs of the user. In most cases, the packages include the software and soundcard, so all you have to do is turn it on. Compared to the cost when all these components are purchased separately, you will come out ahead of the game.

Mixer/Mixing Board

This is where a lot of people mess up. I say "mixer" and you automatically think "DJ mixer," but what you need is a mixing board designed for recording, *not* live performance. It must have at least 4 buses, 2 aux, and 2 outputs. Most importantly, it must have a decent mic pre-amp and phantom power built in.

Microphone

It's a simple concept. If you want your vocals to sound like shit, then buy a shitty microphone. If you want the best, then that's what you buy: The best. This is another area where it is not wise to be a cheap-ass, unless of course you want to sound like shit. Look to spend between $300 and $1,000 for a good-sounding condenser microphone. All microphones are not created equal...

The first mistake that new producers make is that they assume that all microphones are the same. Microphones have many different functions, as well as different sound-shaping aspects to them. Each microphone has its special purpose and no one microphone is a complete problem solver despite what they may say. Remember, if it sounds like shit going in, it will sound like shit coming out, so choose a microphone that best suits your needs. As I said before, there are several different types of microphones to pick from all depending on application. For instance, a dynamic mic is a non-powered mic, used for live sound like a concert of showcase. They possess a rugged sound that is awesome for performing live but terrible for studio use. A condenser mic is a powered mic with a high-end sensitivity which is essential in capturing the crispness of a performance in a studio recording. The condenser mic is powered from either an external power source by the use of phantom power from a mixing board or powered by a battery or stand alone phantom power supply. In the studio, the condenser microphone is the clear choice, but if money is tight, a dynamic microphone can still get the job done in its absence.

Also, do not cut costs on the microphone cable; it's nearly as important as the mic itself for good sound quality.

Add-Ons

Depending on what your goal is, I recommend these items to complete your sound lab:

Sampler/Drum Machine—My favorite is the AKAI MPC 2000/2000 XL.

Keyboard/Sound Module—Most hip-hop producers use the Korg Triton. It has phat sounds and tons of potential for creating new ones, as well as filters, and sampling. Also, check out the Yamaha Motif and the Roland Fantom series.

Turntable—As a DJ, I recommend the Technics SL 1200, but those joints are expensive. If you want to use it to sample your pop's old records, just use any turntable that doesn't hum or buzz, and buy a decent needle.

Studio Monitors

Protect your greatest asset (your ears) and buy a good set of studio monitors that are powered. This way, you won't have to worry about matching the correct amplification with the speakers, because it's already been done by the manufacturer.

Additional Tips and Tricks
Akai MPC 2000 XL-Midi Production Center

The Akai MPC has come a long way since the days of the MPC 60, but this is still one of the most-often used machines in hip-hop production. It is an extremely powerful sampling drum machine / phrase sampler and one of the easiest MIDI sequencers to use on the market.

One of the phattest features of the MPC is that you can make your own sounds and chop up and convert any sample into stereo or mono sounds. It also offers tight filtering capabilities that can give your sounds the gritty low-fi feel of the older models.

Tip: Buy yourself a zip drive for storage and fully expand the memory.

Trick: If you want your drums to bang hard, first you must start with a clean sound and then push the gain to the maximum without distorting the signal.

Warning: Never compress or EQ the sound before you record it.

Once you have named your sample, go to the trim function and make sure that you have truncated the beginning and ending of the sound. Now, while still in the trim function, press the Parameters button and turn the level of the sound to 200. It's that simple. Now your sounds will hit so hard you'll need a hearing aid.

Bonus Trick: Say, for example, you have a kick drum sample that is mad tight, but for some reason it just doesn't hit the way you want it to. Here's the solution: Simply double up the sounds. In each drum pad assignment, there is the option to trigger two additional sounds simultaneously. What you're going to do is dig through your library and load up another kick drum sound that has a loud thumping feel to it, but with no particular sample distinction. For example, an 808 drum machine sample will work perfectly. First assign your main kick to a drum pad, and then assign your 808 kicks to the very next pad. Now, go into the program section of your machine and trigger the two sounds. If you look closely, you will see that each drum sound has a distinctive number assigned to its drum pad. It reads something like this: **Note: 37=Snd:kick,** while the other pad will read **Note: 36=Snd:808kick.** Directly beneath this info it reads **Mode: Normal.** What you want to do is move the cursor to this mode and turn the knob until you read: **Simult also play note:—/off.** Now move the cursor to the "off" mode and turn it until you see the number 36. What you have done is assign both drums to play on the first drum pad, so every time you trigger the first kick, the 808 will trigger at the exact same time. For fine-tuning, adjust the sound level and tune, and filter the sample to your liking. Now go hit 'em in the head with those drums!

Build Your Lab

Every producer has a favorite piece of equipment that he/she uses for all his or her songs. The days of using the Akai MPC are just about over. Nowadays, cats are making hot-ass tracks on just about anything. Even though I swear by the AKAI MPC 2000, it's no longer the only game in town. Computers have taken over the beat-making process to nearly the same extent that they have the rest of the world. For a small amount of cash, an up-and-coming producer can put together a phat-sounding recording studio that rivals any high-priced traditional recording studio. I mean, it's time we kept this shit real: It's supposed to be all about the talent.

As I said in other chapters, when I think of the crap I started out on, it brings tears to my eyes. Nevertheless, I still managed to make some hot beats. You can clearly hear the difference in the level of sound quality between my tracks now and my tracks then. In all honesty, it boils down to your ears and how well you use them. To my amazement, I have heard tracks recorded on an old-ass four-track recorder that sounded like they were recorded in a million-dollar recording studio. On the other hand, I have heard tracks recorded in million-dollar recording studios that sounded like they were recorded on a four-track in someone's closet.

Also in previous chapters, I gave away little tidbits of information on how to keep your game tight. But the most important advice I can give you is to protect your ears. Your ears are your moneymakers. If you fuck them up, you might as well shoot yourself in the dome piece because your career is as good as dead. Can you hear me now? Do not, and I repeat, do not buy cheap speakers or cheap headphones. I know it looks cool, but don't even drive around in your car pumping the radio for the neighborhood to hear. You will ruin your biggest asset, and piss off your neighbors. A little extra cash now will save you millions in the future. Also do not listen to music through a distorted speaker or headphone set. Always invest in the best. There are plenty of other ways to conserve loot when you need to. It's a major sacrifice, I know, but you can't be a cheapskate all your life. Research what is out there. Don't let some salesperson at your local music store sell you on some bull or whatever speakers he happens to have in stock at the time. Talk to people in the business; call around to different recording studios and speak to the head engineer and ask for a recommendation. Pick up a copy of *EQ* or *Mix* magazine and actually read a few of the articles to find out what the industry is using. Then treat yourself; don't cheat yourself.

After doing all the research that you possibly can, take the time to put a studio together that is best suited to your production style. It makes no sense to buy an electric guitar when you do not know how to play it. Use common sense and don't impulse-buy. Also stay away from pieces of equipment that are all-in-one units. Some producers swear by them, but I'd avoid them like the plague. If it's an all-in-one unit, that means it's a combo mixer/recorder/digital editor/sampler, all wrapped up in a neat little package and served up to you for an attractive price. It cannot possibly be as good as each of these pieces individually and still be affordable. Hey, they have to cut costs somewhere. Don't get it twisted, they do serve a purpose and if that's all you can afford, then by all means buy it. Avoid it whenever possible, if you can.

Many times throughout this book I have repeated myself, but repetition serves as a learning tool. So here we go again: Do not buy more equipment than you can handle. If you go out and purchase a bunch of shit that is going to take you twenty years to learn how to use, what sense does that make? How productive would it be if you could not use your gear to produce? The objective here is to buy modular pieces that have growth capability and that are universally compatible. The world was not created in a day so don't expect to build your lab in one. Take time out to master your craft, and utilize your gear to the fullest extent.

I also highly recommend that if you don't already know, learn about the concept of MIDI and how it works. MIDI is the backbone of musical programming. Every hip-hop producer must become a master of programming. Basically, MIDI is a language that allows all of your sound modules to talk to one another so they can be programmed. MIDI allows your sounds to be played in sync, using a master tempo. A master tempo is generated from a sequencing device, e.g. a drum machine, sequencer, computer, instrument, etc., which communicates with each individual instrument module, telling it what sounds to play, and in what sequence (order) to play them. Just as a live band plays together in sync, each instrument plays in time to the tempo or beat, which is kept by the drummer or drum machine. The sequencer keeps time for the producer, just like a drummer in a band.

Okay, I know this sounds real technical, but you need to learn it if you are going to learn how to produce. When I first started, I sampled everything. I hadn't learned how to play the keyboard yet. Even if you never intend to learn how to play keyboard, you still need to know how to sequence in order to trigger samples. Don't be intimidated if you are not a keyboard player; if you have a good idea of how to manipulate sound and have an ear for melody, you will easily pick it up along the way. If worse comes to worse, you can always take a couple of piano lessons.

Creating for the First Time

It's *alive*...Now that you have created your sound lab, you probably feel like Dr. Frankenstein; or better yet, Dr. Funkenstein (Parliament). I bet you're all hyped-up and ready to go and release some of the many crazy ideas flowing through your brain. By now anticipation is making your blood boil and your skin itch, but be patient.

Well, young Jedi, it's time to get to work on those monster tracks. In other words, kid, it's time to get crunk. All of the homework is done. You've checked your competition, and shit is hot right now. What'cha gonna do, I said what'cha gonna do? You can run and hide in your studio and pray for a miracle, or you can get out there and start swinging like Tyson. Maybe you'll kick some ass, or maybe you'll get your ass kicked. Either way, you gotta dive in head first because if you don't, you could be the hottest producer no one has ever heard of. Listen, you have to test your stuff out somewhere, so don't be scared to be heard. Learn to take criticism with a grain of salt. You can take it or leave it. It's up to you, but keep in mind that you want to be innovative. Let your imagination run wild, but stay within the musical parameters that have been set for the times. How do you think P. Diddy stays at the top? Give the people what they want and, believe me, they will never let you down. Be careful about changing too much, because people don't like too much change at once. You have to spoon-feed them like babies. Over the years, I have learned that it is unnecessary to reinvent the wheel: You just need to make a better one. I've also learned that people will love you; people will hate you. You can't please everyone and niggahs in the music business are fickle as hell. Let them do them, and you just do you. Either way, get out there and get your tracks heard.

4

THE GAME PLAN: ASSEMBLE YOUR TEAM

*H*ut one, hut two, hut three... hike! Now that the ball is in play, what'cha gonna do, playa? Well, the answer is to run for the end zone and never look back. It's game time. You've done all the hard work laying down the tracks; you've hit the streets in search of artists; you've even snuck your way into some pretty exclusive industry parties, managing to cop a business card or two. So what now, you ask? Well, my friend, it's time to put the wheels into motion and begin to surround yourself with an all-star team.

The Artist

The artist is a very important piece of the puzzle. He or she can make the critical difference between a good-sounding track and a hit song. It depends on what kind of deal you are seeking but it is always a good idea to have at least one artist in your stable. You can never tell when an A&R scout will be feeling your tracks and want to hear what an artist would sound like over your beats. It can make the difference between a production job and a production deal.

Sorry if I am confusing you with what I am telling you in this chapter; I still feel exactly the same way about dealing with artists as I did in Chapter 2, *Producer or Beat-Maker*—who needs them? Well, you do, but what you don't need is the constant source of headaches and aggravation they cause, unless you're experienced in managing attitudes and prima donnas (or maybe you're just a fool glutton for punishment; only you can decide that). But either way, try to deal with as few artists as creatively possible. Of course the reverse of this is if the artist is already signed to a label and you are getting a fat-ass paycheck to go along with the headaches. If that is the case, just go out and buy some expensive aspirin and call it a day.

The Producer (You)

Being a producer is like being the master of the musical universe. Being a hip-hop producer is like being the master of the ghetto universe. You get to deal with all types of personalities in this business and this crap can work your nerves if you let it. There are no rules to this game and you will come across people who will try to make up a few rules of their own. Just be prepared for anything, including offers of drugs, cash, and plenty of free sex. I'm not trying to preach to you about anything, because I have been guilty a time or two or three of partaking in the festivities. But over the years, you tend to learn from your mistakes. Despite what people say, business and pleasure don't mix. Just ask Bobby and Whitney, Ike and Tina, and anyone who ever signed a deal with a shady-ass record label. Either way, the key to succeeding in this game is to always be on your toes and prepared for anything. Always stay in control of your situation, or your situation will control you.

Learning to Organize

Your first order of business should be to create a sort of Rolodex of talent which you can utilize as a pool of resources at your command. For example, every time you come across an artist or musician who you feel is talented, take down their phone number and ask them if they would be interested in earning a few bucks recording demos or playing riffs for you to sample. If the money in your pocket is low and you find yourself in need of some help, ask if they are willing to barter (exchange) their services for studio time or maybe your producing services. This way everybody wins.

The cool thing about hiring artists or musicians to demo your songs is that you can utilize their talents without having a long-term commitment. This concept is known as work-for-hire. Of course you are going to need a work-for-hire agreement, which I have provided for you in the resource section of this book. In short, it is a simple contract stating that Artist X promises to provide services for Producer Y for Song XYZ. Being that the artist or musician has little involvement other than performing a musical service, which you pay them for, they don't receive any other compensation than the money you agreed to pay them for their services rendered.

The Attorney (Lawyer)

The attorney, or as they are more commonly known as lawyers (or better yet, liars), serve many different purposes in the world of music and are certainly an necessary evil. Some attorney's shop the material of the artist they represent to record companies and music publisher because this guarantees them a paycheck. They can help you navigate through all the red tape, legal mumbo jumbo, and bureaucracy the industry can toss your way. They translate language that may seem comprehensively overwhelming (fucking crazy) into plain English so that you can understand it. The vast majority of them are corrupted and are ethically deviant; the truth for them is always based on their perception and they sure know how to bend it. Experts in manipulation, they can make the difference between going to the studio or going to jail, just ask Slick Rick, Ol' Dirty Bastard, and Shine. These guys make millions a year off the sweat of their clients whether negotiating an album deal or a prison release, they're still getting paid the big bucks, so don't hire one until you absolutely need one.

The Manager

This next topic is a little complicated due to the extreme levels of shadiness that these people may be associated with. The official definition of a manager is someone who handles the business aspect of your musical career, whether you are an artist or producer. They serve as middlemen between you and the music industry. Managers are supposed to guide your music career based on their vast expertise in their field.

That's bull. Most managers usually only manage to steal from you, lie to you, and totally screw up your career. But if you want to succeed in the music industry, you definitely need one. Despite the fact that some are bloodsucking leeches with no morals, ethics, or scruples, managers are a necessary evil.

Manager's Compensation

A decent manager will accept a fee ranging from ten to twenty-five percent of your total income derived from music (the industry standard is twenty percent). In exchange, they will represent your talents and serve as your mouthpiece. Though managers are masters of creating and maintaining relationships, what they actually do is subject to question. Most of them have separate hidden agendas. Some will find you work and some will not. Some will collect monies on your behalf; again, others will not. Basically, what their actual duties are falls into a gray area, which gets fuzzier by the minute. Most importantly, they are your employees. In other words, they work for you; you do not work for them. Why artists fail to understand this I will never know, so don't let some slick-talking manager make you his bitch. Believe me, they will try if you let them.

Power of Attorney

The biggest mistake artists can make is to give their managers "power of attorney." This means that they give their managers total control over their careers. Power of attorney gives the manager the power to sign deals on your behalf, write and cash checks on your behalf, and, worse of all, the right to incur debts on your behalf. All of this as a result of you signing a document that gives the manager your ass. Some managers will even go as far as to explain—or, should I say, lie—that this is beneficial to your career. Bullshit! They will tell you that giving them power of attorney over you will take some of the pressure off your neck, allowing you to focus on being creative. Again, bullshit! Stay on top of your game. You better know what's going on before you end up like a Hammer, dead-ass broke.

Well, I could go on for pages with endless management horror stories, but by now you should have the gist. Play it smart and always have an active role in your career. Whether dealing with artists, musicians, or managers, you must watch your back, homie. Remember that you are the coach, and just like a coach, you have to understand how to motivate your team (artists) effectively. So never lose focus and, more importantly, never give up control of your team. Ask yourself where Michael Jordan would be today if it hadn't been for the guidance of a great coach.

5

GET OUT THERE:
MARKET AND PROMOTE YOUR PRODUCT

Invent, evaluate, and infiltrate and if that doesn't work, start all over and do it again. The whole idea behind this concept is to be flexible. Face it, nobody has ever heard of your ass anyway, so what difference does it make to you if you have to change what you're doing in order to get your foot in the door? I swear, I've seen so many artists straight-up fuck themselves out of a deal because they were unwilling to bend even a little. Don't misunderstand me. I'm not saying bust out the Hammer pants, but you have to keep an open mind about the whole thing. If record labels are signing southern krunk rappers and you sound like a fresh-out-of-jail MC on some old Kris Kross-type shit, then maybe that should be your first indication that it's high time you changed your game plan. Look at it from the record label's perspective. Then ask yourself (or maybe you should ask a total stranger), "Am I marketable? Do I have a product that American consumers cannot live without?"

On the real, you don't have to be that damn extreme, but keep it real with yourself. If you are a fat bald guy in your mid-thirties rapping about your struggles as a suburban mailman and you got your shirt off in your promo picture, playa, your shit is incorrect. Go with the times, take a minute to research the competition, and then model yourself after someone who is successful in the music business. And I don't mean *one-hit wonders or overnight sensations, either.* Artists who have ten or more years in the game know exactly how to keep the buying public coming back for more. For example, artists like LL Cool J and Busta Rhymes are always successful because they are constantly developing and evolving as artists. If you want to stay in the game, you gotta play the game. Remember that very few artists get to make the rules.

Okay, you're fresh out of the studio with your new CD and you know labels are gonna sign you, right? Wrong. Unless P. Diddy is your uncle, labels are not looking to sign someone they never heard of. You gotta get your product some exposure. I don't care if you live in backwater Mississippi or Fucknut County, South Dakota, there is someone else in your town who likes the same music you like. So, there has to be at least one club, restaurant, bar, or even rodeo that will let you perform there for free. Yes, I said *free*. Don't think somebody's gonna pay to hear MC KEEPINGITREAL and DJ HARDCOREKILLANIGGAH if they've never heard of you before.

Time For Promotion

Guess what? Its time to go to Kinko's (or your local print shop), and print up all the promotional merchandise you can afford. Flyers, business cards, t-shirts, and posters...whatever it takes to promote yourself. Then literally plaster your town or city with this merchandise. Create a buzz about your music. Hook up with known DJs (radio or party) from your area and ask them to play your song on their radio show or next mix tape. That's usually an excellent way to be heard. Offer to do promos for their radio show or mix tape in exchange for airplay. If that doesn't work, just offer them some money or whatever they're into. Remember, don't take no for an answer, but don't try to kick their asses if they refuse to help you, either. There is a fine line between being persistent and being annoying: Learn where the line is and remember it.

In addition, try to have the local newspaper write an article about your group and where you will be performing. Find out what hip-hop-related shows will be taking place in your area and who is doing the promotion. That's the person with the power to skyrocket your career into stardom. It has been my experience as a promoter that the small-venue shows and club appearances really boost the careers of local talent. Normally, if a big-name act is playing a local spot, they usually don't perform until at least two or three in the morning. You can always count on seeing one or two opening acts perform before the main show. This is where you fit in.

Become An Opening Act

So, it's been settled. Group XYZ has been booked and is scheduled to perform at the local nightclub in your city. Through good networking and a little luck, you have managed to get on the bill as the opening act. It's show time and the opportunities are about to start pouring in. The show's headliner is a multi-platinum hip-hop group that has the hottest record on the radio since the Beatles. The local radio station has been running non-stop commercials promoting the show and is also the show's main sponsor. The radio station's best DJ is going to host the show and a slew of other radio and record company personnel will be on hand to critique the performance.

The night of the show finally arrives and the main act rolls into town with an entourage bigger than Hammer's. Roll out the red carpets, because the sky is the limit. Everyone is getting the star treatment and you're eating it up. Now that the infamous green room is packed to capacity, here is your chance to rub elbows with the bigwigs. The odds are that someone in the room can help you get where you want to be. The music business is quite competitive and even though everything is all good, everyone in the industry has their eye on each other's jobs. If you observe the scenery and do a little strategic questioning, you will get the down-low on what is really happening in the industry.

Just as the world is round, I can guarantee that someone in the group has his or her own production company or label. If you think about all the artists and producers who got their start by piggybacking off another artist, it's startling. So if these industry cats are scouting for talent, they will definitely be keeping a watchful eye on your performance. Managers also always have their antennas up, trying to tune into the hottest new talent. But if all else fails, you can at least get your hands on a business card, and that's always a solid lead. Watch the crowd for a person who seems really interested in what's happening backstage, because that is usually the A&R person. Keep your eyes and ears open. You never know whom you might meet.

Six minutes to go until you're on. Suddenly you get amnesia, your throat is dry, and your palms are sweaty. But you become calm and ready to get it on. Here you go, kid; tear up the fucking club!

In a snap, it's over. You did it; the best performance of your career. Everyone was feeling you. The club was filled with industry folks and all eyes were on you. If the rest of the show was a success, the next day the radio station will be talking about the show every time they play XYZ's hit record.

That's when the DJ who hosted the show starts bragging about how he discovered your group and takes the credit for your talented performance. Right about now, you are probably saying to yourself, "What the fuck? This DJ doesn't even know me and he's taking the credit for discovering my group!" Look, homie, don't sweat the small stuff and just remember that everyone wants to be on the winning team. Plus, it doesn't matter if they even knew you like that or not, because this is your chance to work the discovery angle.

Capitalize On After-Show Publicity

Now pay close attention to what I am about to drop. You and your boys spend the next week or so calling the radio station to request songs and info about your group. Call all day and night. Get your friends, neighbors, ex-girlfriends, and your babies' mamas to call. Even though the radio station doesn't have a copy of your CD, they cannot stand to let their listeners down. They will make every effort to get in contact with you in order to cop one.

At a minimum you'll get a little airplay during a mix show or an interview by the DJ who proclaimed to have discovered you. Don't expect the radio station to add your song to their play list because their music is usually programmed by their parent company, but stranger things have happened.

So, in conclusion, with a little elbow grease, some light ass-kissing and some serious prayer, you can manage to get your music out there and create a buzz for your material.

6

THE HOOK-UP:
NETWORK FOR OPPORTUNITIES

ow many times have you heard the old saying, "It's not what you know, it's who you know"? Probably more than you care to admit. The truth of the matter is that this is some true shit, especially in the music business. Think about it: One day you're riding in your car. You turn on the radio to hear the DJ popping some yang about how he got his hands on an exclusive new song that's gonna take the world by storm. To your major disappointment, the record stinks worse than a pile of hot garbage on a summer's day. Without thinking, you say to yourself, "How the fuck did they get on the radio?"

Sound familiar, huh? Well, it should. Every day some whack-ass singer, rapper, or entertainer extraordinaire slips through the cracks—like a hungry roach on a mission—and onto your radio dial. This epidemic can sometimes seem overwhelming, as if somewhere in the world there is a factory manufacturing whack-ass rappers and singers. Right now, go to any corner in any hood. You will find cats that can spit better lyrics than half the people you hear on the radio, but they don't have a record deal. Go to any gospel church on a Sunday (it's a good place to find R&B singers), grab a seat in the back row, and listen for a few hours. I guarantee you will find the next Mariah or Whitney. It makes you wonder: If there is so much unsigned talent in the world, then why are they playing such bullshit on the radio? Well, the main reason these whack artists make it to the radio is that the artist has managed to make a lot of connections. Though the sophisticated folks in the music business world call it networking, it is nothing more than good, old-fashioned hooking-up. Shake a hand, make a connection, make a deal. Remember, everybody knows somebody who has a friend who's got a cousin whose neighbor works in the record business.

I personally have used this method to get a meeting with an A&R person I didn't know. Other times I just happened to be in the right place at the right time. Your hook-up may only be a handshake away, so start shaking hands. It takes balls to walk up to a total stranger and ask for something, especially if you are a nobody. But if you got balls, use them. Ninety percent of the time you will be brushed off like a little peon, but there's always that ten percent when someone will be willing to listen to what you have to say.

Stop for a second, though. Don't attempt this if your shit is not prepared. If you don't have a current demo CD and a bio on hand, don't even think about it. Spare yourself the heartache and pain. Keep in mind that a hungry mouth gets fed and a quiet mouth goes hungry. Perfect your schmoozing skills. It takes time to know what to say and when to say it, but it's not that hard to accomplish.

Personally, I hate it when people approach me and they have no idea what to say or how to ask me for help. They tend to trip over their own tongues and end up sounding like babbling idiots. What I hate the most are the been-there-done-that types, who run their mouths like they got verbal diarrhea. They go on and on, and always about nothing. Use charm, be reserved, and respect the person's space and time. Say only what is necessary to pique their interest, but without turning them off. Spare yourself the embarrassment and forget about performing your entire collected works for the person live. Don't expect to conduct business at a nightclub or concert, especially if you are not part of the elite inner circle. Half of these record-company types won't remember you the next day anyway, unless, of course, they are completely impressed by you.

Pay Your Dues

Enough said. Let me talk about the topic of hunger. Hunger should be used as a tool to strive and gain ground in your journey to success. Hunger is a never-say-die attitude and a willingness to do whatever it takes to get shit done. So if we all agree that hungry people get to eat, then why is it that so many artists are starving?

My guess is laziness. This past decade has bred some of the laziest artists the game has ever known. Cats who started rapping on Monday think that they should have a million-dollar deal by Friday, but they haven't put down the blunt long enough to put in the work. A starving artist has no other choice but to be resourceful. You have to be a jack-of-all-trades if you want to make it into the inner circle. If you aren't willing to work your ass off without a paycheck or a simple thank-you, then this is not the job for you.

Even someone as powerful as P. Diddy, a.k.a. Sean Combs, started out at the bottom of the ladder. Puff started his career as an intern at Uptown Records. He traveled many hours to work under someone who was obviously 100 times less intelligent than him, and for absolutely free. Puffy worked hard to earn the chance to enter the inner circle, and now he owns it. Shit, I interned at RCA/BMG for two years before getting recognized. Getting up at the ass-crack of morning, spending my own money on the two-hour commute from Long Island to Manhattan, just so I could learn how to use the music business to my advantage and get my feet wet. In this business, you have to be willing to sacrifice your time, money, and energy in order to get your Timbs in the door.

Think of the record industry as an egg. The yolk represents the people in the industry, and the white represents the people who are trying to get into the industry. The divisions of power and influence are greatly mismatched. As an artist, you are at an automatic disadvantage. There is also a definite distinction of separatism between the haves and the have-nots.

So if the record industry is like an egg, only when you decide to mix it up will you get satisfying results. Scramble the yolk and act like a politician. Shake hands and kiss babies if you gotta. Why do you think they call it politicking, or poly'n? Mix it up and mingle, crash the industry functions (whether you are invited or not), and learn to think on your feet. If the front door is locked, then knock on the back door. Slip the bouncer a $50; it may well be worth it for a chance to hobnob with the inner circle.

Oh, and by the way, kill the complaining. Some of my old associates used to complain all the time about how they never knew what was going on in the industry. They felt like they were always out of the loop. I would constantly remind them that they could not expect to know what was going on in the industry if they were not actively involved in it. They expected the A&R rep to come knock on their studio door and say, "Hey, man, you want some money?" And for this sole reason, I constantly stress the importance of getting involved in the business. When I first started, a wise man once told me that if I wanted to be in the music business, I had to make it my business to know music.

You know that extra time you spend sitting around, complaining that such-and-such has a record deal and you don't? Well, that time can be spent at a label or production company, working as an intern or volunteer (for free) and keeping your ear to the ground. Almost every record label has a promotions department and that department has some form of street team that usually handles the promotions for record stores, clubs, concerts, and industry parties. If that's not an excellent way to get started, then I don't know what is.

Industry Friendships

Lastly, I will discuss the word "friendship." Whodini described it best when he said, "A friend is somebody you judge for yourself." Don't be a fool. You have no friends in the industry, only allies. These people are bound to you for one reason only: Money, and how much, and for how long you can keep their pockets fat. If you think everything is all buddy-buddy, just wait until your next record doesn't sell, then see where all of your so-called friends are. What, you thought TLC was bullshitting? Music is a business before it is anything else, so money will always be the greatest factor. Fuck musical integrity, honesty, and fair play. Get in, get paid, and get out. Haul ass to the next payday while you got the chance. Don't get it wrong, there are still a few honest people in the business, but usually they are new and it does not take them long to become influenced by the money and the power. God knows I have been, but the key to success is to keep things in perspective. I can truly say I have some friends in the game and we share a common respect. But the bottom line is always about the money, never the friendship. Therefore, in the greater scheme of things, I look at them as my allies rather than my friends. Jointly we have agreed to make money, and tons of it.

I must say it again: Think on your feet. Not everybody is out to fuck you with no Vaseline, but too many people out there *are*. One time I set up a deal with a big-time producer/artist-type to remix (or should I say reproduce) about half of his album. My partner at the time and I decided to take the offer, and I negotiated a deal for $30,000 for six remixes, which excluded studio time and mixing. As additional payment, they gave us three multitrack machines to be used for transfers, worth about $9,000 total. The grand total compensation was approximately $40,000, give or take a penny. The only catch was that we had to do it in "one week's time." Being that we were producers and engineers, it wasn't going to be a problem.

The producer/artist became so impressed by our work ethic and talent that he wanted to scrap some of the other songs from his album and pay us to write/produce new songs as their replacements. Up for the challenge and the sheer love of money, we gladly accepted the offer. The conditions were agreed upon the commencement of work, but no formal paperwork was ever drawn up or signed. Mistake number one. Even though we were paid in full for the first deal, we should have signed on the dotted line before we began the work on the second deal. Caught up in the level of attention the project required and the high demand for its timely completion, we left it up to the client's attorney to provide us with the necessary paperwork. Mistake number two.

During this time we began to build a working friendship with the client and his staff. The client, who is a multi-millionaire, constantly spent money on meals and entertainment on our behalf, all the while telling us he believed in our talents and wanted us to join his team. As he put it, "Let's be a family." Now I don't know about you, but to us that shit sounded like pure hustle. Family? We had just met him the week before. Needless to say, we wanted to see how the whole thing would play itself out, so we went along for the ride. Mistake number three.(We shouldn't have wasted our time.)

Well, the closer we got to the deadline, the fuzzier the verbal deal got. Excuses were flowing like shit through a goose. "Oh! My lawyer is out of town…" "My singers need to have more of an active role in the creative process." Pure bullshit! Soon our happy family became dysfunctional enough to get a spot on the Jerry Springer show.

At that point we were tired of playing games, so we called his bluff. All of a sudden our new best friend had to leave town on business, leaving behind his staff to clean up his mess.

When the smoke cleared, though, we came out ahead of the game. All the songs were recorded at our studio and so we got paid for our time. Also, we retained ownership of the songs we wrote and produced, featuring his artist singing on them. As a result, we could shop the songs for a publishing deal because we owned the copyrights. Six months later the album dropped. They ended up using only three of the six songs we remixed, and therefore we got paid for some old tracks we had lying around that they didn't even use.

The downside was that in retaliation for the botched deal, they screwed us by not giving us a co-production credit for the songs we reproduced. Instead they credited us as additional arrangers and programmers, but not as co-producers. The fucked-up thing was that by the time we were able to take legal action against their blatant breach of contract, the album had already gone platinum. It would have been pointless to change the liner notes after the fact.

Chalk it up to experience. Sometimes the game is unfair. As I said, it would have been pointless to sue them after the fact. He was a multimillionaire and we were not, enabling him to tie us up in court so long that when it was all over, we would probably have to pay him. This was a valuable lesson that neither my partner nor I soon forgot. Instead of getting discouraged, though, we just learned to tighten up our game, and we moved on. An old army sergeant of mine used to say to me, "In this world you got to be two things: Flexible and willing to execute." He actually called it "flexicute." You have to be able to flexicute at the drop of a dime in this game, if you want to get ahead.

Take the time to realize what you're getting yourself into, and then remember: In this business, you have no friends, just allies. Learn to utilize their power and influence and they will serve you well. Game recognizes game.

7

GET MONEY

Right about now you are excited about becoming a big-time hip-hop producer, touring the world with fine-ass women on your arm, big cars, all-night parties, and mad cash in your bank account. Wake up, kid, this ain't a video. You gotta get up, get out there, and make it happen. You need to know how to get paid and stay paid. Your piece of the pie is out there, but getting your slice is gonna take some serious doing. So before you go out and put that new car on your mama's credit, you need to know and understand the basic mechanics of how the producer gets his money.

How Payment Works

As a hip-hop producer, a record label or an artist usually hires you, but no matter which of the two hires you, as a producer you are entitled to an advance.

The Advance

An advance is monies that are paid to you either from the record company or artist before you start the record-making process. Think of it as a loan on a product that has not hit the market yet, but some expert thinks will do well. This loan comes from the money that the record company decided to spend on the artist's project. What this means is that all of these monies handed out in advance by the record company must be recouped or collected before you get any additional compensation (loot) owed to you from future record sales. Simply put, before you get your check, the loan must be paid. The cool thing is that once the record company gets all of the loot they kicked out for the artist's project, the producer gets paid retroactively from the sale of the very first record.

Before you start thinking you're about to get broke off, cool your jets, kid. Keep in mind that just because you may be entitled to an advance does not necessarily mean you will get one. But in this case, we will remain optimistic. Advances can range from as low as $500 or as high as $150,000. It all depends on your status in the game. As a new hip-hop producer, you should expect your advance to be on the low end. More than likely, expect to be paid under $10,000.

All-In-Recording Budget

Don't sweat it. There are still other ways of getting paid. For example, another way for a producer to get paid is to ask for an All-In-Recording Budget. This is a fund negotiated by the producer that is large enough to record the artist's entire project and still leave the producer with a little leftover cash to wet his beak. With an All-In-Recording Budget there is no need for a producer advance, therefore eliminating the funds that have to be recouped by the record company. The whole objective of this arrangement is to produce the project under budget and break yourself off a nice little chunk of change, which is usually larger than what the record company was going to hit you off with in the first place. This method has been quite successful for my associates and I, but it is extremely difficult to manage if you have no previous business experience. I recommend that as a new producer you should not even consider the idea. I was just giving you a little future information to grow on. Play at your own risk, playa.

It has been my experience that, when dealing with smaller labels, it is a smart move to get as much money as you can upfront, even if this means you have to take lower producer royalty points. A lot of these smaller companies are fly-by-night bullshit ex-drug dealer or pro athlete operations that usually fold within a year or so. You must take the money and run, especially if you think that you may never see a royalty check from these clowns.

Retain Your Rights

Please remember this: *Never Sell Your Tracks Outright.* It doesn't matter how much they offer you. Always hang on to a piece of your track, even if you never see a royalty check. If by some miracle the record jumps off, you want to have something to show for it. Even if it's just a producer's credit on a hit record, you'll have something to use as leverage on the next deal. Once again, *Never Sell Your Tracks Outright. Never Sell Your Tracks Outright. Never Sell Your Tracks Outright.* "Even if they're offering you a million dollars?" (Bear in mind that they think they can make ten-million dollars off it.) "No. Never."

You would be a complete jackass if you sold it outright. The potential to make future money is right in your face, but you have to decide when to hold 'em and when to fold 'em.

Quick story: A fellow hip-hop producer, who is a friend of mine, sold a track outright to a big-name rapper/record company owner for about $2,500.00. Needless to say, the record blew up and is now considered a classic party record, played by DJs all over the world. For whatever reason, he took the money and waived all of his rights to future royalties. He screwed himself out of any entitlement to that record whatsoever. To make matters even worse, he wasn't even credited as the producer on the record, so he couldn't add it to his discography.

Letter of Direction

More recently, there has been a trend building in the industry where record companies are dealing less with the daily mechanics of making records and developing artists. They have left these tasks up to the artists themselves and their management teams. As a result, the artists and their people are now responsible for the hiring and payment of their producers. Most artists I know stay blunted ninety percent of the time, and I am pretty damn sure that they don't have an accounting degree from Harvard, nor do their managers. Plus, these artists can be as shady as some of these bullshit-ass labels. Most of them can barely stay on top of their own financial situation, so how in the hell does somebody expect them to keep track of yours?

There is a light at the end of the tunnel, though. The way around this crap is to demand that the label the artist is signed to pay you money directly. It is sort of choosing the lesser of two evils, but at least the record labels have people who know how to use a calculator. What you need to do is send a letter of direction to the record company, instructing them to pay your money directly to you and not to the artist. If your money comes straight to you, the middleman is eliminated and there's less chance of you catching a case for running up on the artist and his crew at the club.

Producer Royalties

I know by now that if you were smart enough to buy this book, at least you grasp the basic concept of what producer royalties (points) are, but if not, don't sweat it; I got you, kid.

Producer royalties are monies earned from the sale of records that you have produced. Every time a consumer purchases music that you have produced, you earn a certain percentage of the profits. As the sales grow, the money begins to add up, and when it reaches a certain amount—come accounting time—you are issued a check. Producer royalties vary from between one-and-a-half percent to three percent for a new producer and six percent and higher for a producer with a big track record.

Now on the other hand, playa, if the artist is already established or the record label has an excellent track record, you might want to opt for a smaller advance and larger producer royalty points. If you go this route, there is very little to be recouped, your royalties are paid to you a whole lot faster and you earn a few more dollars on the back end. A lot of times you will end up doing better than the artist, especially if this is their first record. It's always nice to get a check in the mail while your record is still pumping on the radio and TV.

Each project is on an individual basis and is subject to negotiation, so the bottom line is to negotiate in your favor as much as possible. If you don't catch the big fish the first time out, don't worry 'cause there are a lot of fish in the sea. Just make sure you got a pole. No deal is perfect and there are always some ups and downs, so don't be discouraged. Just learn from each of your experiences and benefit from the experiences of others around you.

8

STAYING PAID

ail to plan, and plan to fail. You've probably heard some old person kicking this shit into your ear nearly all of your life. The truth is that they were absolutely right. In order to succeed, you must plan for success. Planning is a road map for your career. Kool G Rap once said, "I'm on the road to riches." Yeah, so was I, then suddenly the yellow brick road became a dead end. During my sudden rise from poverty, I never took the time out to exercise my fiscal (financial) fitness.

Right now you're probably scratching your head, thinking what in the fuck is he talking about? Pay close attention. I failed to plan for my financial future and it nearly crippled my bank account. I thought that I would be paid royalty checks for the rest of my life, but like so many other washed-up artists, I was dead-ass wrong. Shit, there are so many artists who were once successful in the music biz that the government should have some kind of Federal relief fund, like Hip-Hop Aid or something.

But seriously, this is no laughing matter. Fortunately for me, I was able to parlay my skills and talents into alternative forms of employment in the music industry, other than production. These little "odd jobs" sustained me long enough to get back on track so I could keep producing records. I have done a lot of "odd jobs" in the music industry, and a lot of them paid nothing and were not too glamorous.

This is what it really boils down to: As a student of the music business, you must study basic business practices in order to prepare yourself for success. Barry White confessed that one year he was on welfare, and the following year he made over a million dollars. Many fortunes have been won and lost, empires built and toppled, and families torn apart because of greed for money. It just goes to show that anything can happen in the music biz, and your luck could change from good to bad in an instant. Drug addicts claim that crack is highly addictive; professional athletes profess that playing sports is highly addictive; but neither one can compare with the addiction to money.

The addiction to money was one of the main reasons why I stayed in the music business as long as I did. Like a fiend, I was constantly searching and seeking for the next big opportunity to strike it rich. Money is the sole source of motivation for a lot of people; the entire reason they ever picked up a mic. I can definitely agree with their level of thinking. The first time I got a royalty check for $35,000, I was like, "Holy shit, that's a niggah's whole year's pay," so you can just imagine how I felt when I got a check for $75,000.

Accounting

But what I didn't know—and what you don't know can kill you—was that the record company does not take out the money for your taxes. They leave all that shit up to you. Guess what, that $75,000 was cut down to about $45,000, thanks to good old Uncle Sam.

Most of us slept through high school dreaming about making it big, having a phat ride, and some big-booty hoes, so you know we weren't about to become accountants overnight. Well, the question is, who can you trust to take care of Uncle Sam—because you have to trust someone, right? Shopping for a good accountant is as important as shopping for a record deal. You have to be extremely careful and investigate the accountant's business practices thoroughly. Do background checks, talk to their other clients, and make sure that their credentials are for real. The last thing you need is a problem with the IRS, and I say this to you from experience. Fuck around and you'll be recording albums for the IRS, like Willie Nelson. Do you think I'm joking? You will literally be forced to record an album in order to pay what you owe to Uncle Sam.

DIY Computer Programs

Basic bookkeeping is a business essential. There's about a million and one computer programs on the market that do bookkeeping. My favorite, and the easiest to use, is Quicken. It is also quite affordable and cheaper than a tax attorney. Also, if you have some free time, you could always take an accounting class at a community college for about $150. This is a very small investment that could save you millions in the future.

Every time I hear artists/producers on TV talking about the stupid bullshit they waste their money on, I want to spit up my milk and cookies. A muthafucka will buy fifty cars, but only has one ass to drive them. Let's get real! Don't buy into that ghetto-rich shit. Do you know how the rich get rich and stay rich? Well, it ain't by spending money on stupid shit like cars and mink comforter sets. They make their money by building up their assets.

Assets

Assets are things that you buy that make you money, like real estate, fine art, stocks, and mutual funds. When you spend your money on cars with rims and custom jewelry, you are buying liabilities.

Liabilities

Liabilities are things such as cars, boats, and credit-card debts, or anything that loses you money or causes you to spend money. Don't get it fucked up; rich people have all of the same things, but the difference is that they acquire the assets first, which in turn allows them to buy the toys they want using the profit dollars they earn from their assets.

A Real-World Example

Most artists make a little cash and go out directly and buy extravagant things, many of which they could not have afforded if they were not famous, and if they worked a regular 9-to-5 job. Having incurred such a high level of debt, they are forced to keep making records to keep the bill collectors off their asses. Say an artist gets an album deal for $250,000, $200,000 is spent on making the record and $50,000 is an advance to the artist. Then say he has halfway decent credit and buys a $100,000 car with $20,000 down (just for argument's sake), but he still owes $80,000. Next he takes $20,000 more and puts it down on a $100,000 condo. Now he owes another $80,000, and we haven't even factored in interest rates or taxes (which we will ignore for the purposes of simplicity). Another $10k is spent on jewelry and clothes. Magically, his $50k advance has changed into a whopping $160k in debt. Before he ever sells his first record, he is already $410k in the hole. $410k, you ask? How? Well, I guess you forgot about the $250k spent on the album and artist advance that is both completely recoupable. This means that every dollar spent by the record company on the artist's behalf must be repaid to the record company by monies earned from record sales before the artist gets paid one red cent in artist royalties. Now, by adding the amount of debt that the artist owes to the record company to the amount of debt the artist has incurred personally, the artist would be left with a debt of $410k.

But wait, it gets worse. The album drops and ships gold, which is 500,000 units, but because of returns and reductions it actually only sells about 250,000 units. Let's say the average CD price is about $12.00. Multiply the amount of CDs sold by the amount of units sold, which totals $3-million dollars in sales the artist has earned, right? *Wrong!* The artist gets a mere twelve percent of the total amount. His cut is about $360,000, from which the $250k album cost will be deducted leaving an amount of $110k which is still not bad at all, but the government gets their 35 percent of that amount, leaving him with a final paycheck of $38,500. But because the artist still has a personal debt totaling $160,000, the artist will remain in the hole for $121,500 worth of debt and no real way to pay it back. Sort of makes you want to cry, huh?

Wait a minute. Remember he financed both the house and the car, so he has to make a monthly payment, with interest. Let's see: The car was financed for sixty months (five years), making his monthly payment approximately $1,300, and the condo was financed for fifteen years, with a payment of approximately $640 a month.

It can take up to eighteen months from the time the artist gets his advance until the artist gets paid his first royalty check. During this time period, the artist is on the road doing free promotional tours to support sales of the album and does not have a monthly income, but he has a combined car and house debt of nearly $2,000, plus daily living expenses. Most loan companies begin the repossession and foreclosure process after about three months of non-payment, but they are willing to work with him because he is a rising star. So if we wanted to include penalties and fees, and not to mention the interest, he would really be up shit creek.

By now you should have gotten the point and there really is no reason to continue. The moral of the story is: Learn to think smart. Do not get caught up in the baller lifestyle before you're earning the baller salary.

Judging Production Deals

Now that we have discussed what can happen to an artist when he mismanages his money, let's focus on the producer. The only concrete difference between an artist and a producer is that, as a producer, your percentage rate is usually around three percent. Because this figure is considerably lower than that of an artist, one can only imagine the amount of hot water he could find himself drowning in.

I would like to make one last point. When fishing for the record deal of the century, do not forget about the little fish. The reason this is of such grave importance is that sometimes the success earned from a few small fish, when added together, can be equal to the same amount of success as one great big fish.

This lesson I had to learn the hard way. For many years I told the story about the big fish that got away. This arrogant way of thinking nearly cost me my career. I was just like you once: Hungry, frustrated, and lost in the game with no direction. I was always willing to do whatever it took to get in the game. A DJ gig here, a club appearance here, and a whole lot of fighting for survival in between. For years I tried to shop my own material, but only got marginal results at best. Finally, while I was going to college in Atlanta, I got an opportunity to get off the bench and get some real playing time. I belonged to a rap group that won a spot on tour as the opening act for a big-name rap group. To make a long story short, the tour was a complete success, even though we didn't make much money. We were given the star treatment, and believe me, that shit is the bomb.

After several months on tour, the party was over and it was time to head back to Atlanta. What sucked the most about the tour ending was that even though we were the shit on the road, in the real world we still didn't have a record deal. To make matters worse, we had an infidel in our midst. One of the cats in the group, who had been a shady-ass niggah from the start, decided that he was too big for the group and he was going to quit.

His speedy departure was quite hilarious. I was the group's producer and wrote seventy-five percent of this niggah's rhymes, but he was too big for us. Karma is a muthafucka, because shortly thereafter RCA/BMG wanted to sign us, but there wasn't a group left to sign. Willing to take a chance, I moved back to New York and convinced the executives at RCA/BMG to take a chance on me as an artist/writer/producer.

My manager at the time, the late Barry Yearwood (As-Salaam Aliakum), felt that it was a great career move for me and it would help get in the door. He was absolutely right. RCA/BMG gave me my first major deal as an artist/producer/writer. The first group that I worked with was virtually unknown, but right out of the box they were a huge success, earning themselves a Grammy nomination and over two-million units sold in album sales. There I was, dead smack in the middle of all the glitter and glamour, and I was loving it. I was given the royal treatment; the very best of everything. The paycheck was large—I mean, real large—especially for a first-time producer. But my ass got too spoiled. When the ride was over and the smoke had cleared, I had a huge problem about being humble and getting back to the basics of production. It didn't matter what type of deal I was offered, nothing was good enough for the King. I always used my last deal as a comparison for any deal that was offered to me. None even came close. I swear, ego-tripping is a muthafucka. Labels were offering me projects left and right, and I was turning them down like a nerd at a high-school dance. I couldn't get off my own dick long enough to see what was going on right in front of my face. Eventually time had slipped away and I wasn't working.

That's the reason why there is a small but noticeable gap in my discography timeline. When I finally pulled my head out of my ass long enough to see what was going on around me, I gained a little forward momentum. A remix here, a programmer's gig there, but nothing really major.

Finally, I recaptured the thrill of the hunt and got my shit into high gear. A very trusted and longtime ally of mine made an astonishing observation about my work ethics. He said that he'd noticed I made tons and tons of tracks every week, but I never did anything with them except play them in my car, and what purpose did that serve? After unsuccessfully shopping a track to a label or artist, I would just toss it into my beat archives for later use. What the fuck was I thinking? I could turn around and recycle those old tracks and sell them to someone who wasn't a major player in the game, but who just needed good material to get a deal with. By wasting my material, I was doing myself a huge injustice.

I decided to take his advice. I took all the tracks that were lying around collecting dust and put them onto a CD as one-minute snippets. Then I compiled a price sheet and put them into a neat little package. I called this concept "QUICK BEATS." A lot of times, an artist who is working on a second or third album might be looking for different tracks to demo for his album. They might be budget-conscious and searching for a new producer who doesn't charge an arm and a leg for his beats. Instead of buying one track for $10,000, they might want to buy three tracks for that price. By retaining a producer's royalty rate of three percent per track, and providing that the album hits, you may make more money on the back end. This way you come out ahead of the game, especially if the artist cannot afford to pay $10,000 a track.

In other instances, artists who are up-and-coming or who are shopping a deal for the first time, may be looking to lease (rent) a track for an agreed-upon period of time. In simple terms, this is a rental agreement that allows the artist to record and shop your track for a short period of time, usually six to twelve months. A fee is arranged for the use of the track, as well as the producer's time and effort. These fees are completely negotiable, usually ranging anywhere from $500 to $1,500. After the agreed-upon shopping period has ended and there is no deal signed or pending, the artist must cease and desist using the track. The usage of the track reverts back to the producer to be used in any way he desires. On the other hand, if the artist lands a deal, it is up to the label to negotiate with the producer regarding ownership of the track. In addition, sometimes it might be in the best interests of the producer to sell the track outright to the artist, but this is purely conditional.

The bottom line is to plan ahead and stay focused on the business, as well as the creative aspects of the game. Never lose sight of the reason you are playing: Whether it is for the love of the game, or for the love of money, if you don't stay on top of it, the results can be devastating. Concentrate on developing a good business sense and it will take care of your finances in the long run. There is an old saying that goes, "If you give a man a fish you can feed him for a day, but if you teach a man how to fish he can eat for a lifetime."

Become a fisherman and eat like a king.

9

NO VASELINE:
AVOIDING THE SNAKES AND THIEVES

on't hate the playa, hate the game. There ain't no rules to this, man. It's like the Wild West. All you can do is protect your ass, any way you can. I think that at some point or another I have run into just about every crook in the music industry. These clowns were pretending to be everything under the sun: Managers, lawyers, agents, and record executives. Once I even ran into this idiot who attempted to convince me that he was part of the Sugar Hill Gang. Firstly, I just happened to know who the Sugar Hill Gang were and what they looked like. Secondly, his shiny red suit and Payless shoes were a dead giveaway that his ass was broke. Plus, this dude didn't even own a car. People will throw all kinds of shit at you to divert your attention from your money, including sex. Don't let your little producer get your big producer into some shit you will live to regret. These bloodthirsty wolves are trifling, and they will do whatever they have to do to throw you off your game. You gotta be careful out there.

Getting Burned

I used to know a producer who was really down on his luck and seriously hurting for money. He was doing bad and then his girl threw him out of their crib, so he was living in his car. The saddest part was that he had talent out the ying yang. Everybody was feeling his tracks. Due to the fact that he needed loot so badly, he ended up signing a bad deal with a management company that offered him $15,000. In desperate need of some fast cash to get himself back on his feet, he quickly accepted. As time went by, the management company he signed with got him lots of work, but kept most, if not all, of the money he earned. After deciding he had been getting screwed over for long enough, he hired an accountant to audit the management company's books. What the accountant discovered was that the money they had advanced to the producer had long been recouped, but the producer had never received any additional money for his hard work. He also discovered that the reason they never paid him was that the management company had accounted for every cent they had ever kicked out on the producer's behalf, down to the mileage that they put on their cars when they drove him to the studio. Even trips to the 7/11 for late-night snacks and visits to Mickey D's. See, my man was in such a hurry to get some cash in his hands that he didn't bother to read the contract he signed, so he signed away his life.

The moral of the story is read everything before you sign it. If you don't understand it, have someone who does understand it read it for you. Don't be cheap: If you have to break down and pay a lawyer to read it, then, homie, those are the breaks. Can't be cheap all your life, right? The money you spend today could very well save you from getting ass-raped, jailhouse-style, tomorrow.

Danger, danger... Be on the lookout for this kind of idiot... I'm talking about the Instant Homie. This is the worst kind of person to deal with in the business and here's why. These types of people meet you, and instantly fall in love with you. All of a sudden it's bam, "Now we are buddies"-type shit. They want to work with you, but they keep avoiding the topic of money, talking about how you need to start a family and grow in the business together. Pure bullshit. It wouldn't be so bad if it was an artist, producer, or manager, someone on the same level as you, but this crap usually jumps out of the mouths of A&R executives and artists who have the power to make or break your career. They are only looking to get their side hustle on.

What all this boils down to is that if you start some type of partnership with them, they can exploit the shit out of your talents without paying you because you're a partner in some half-ass venture. Run as fast as you humanly can. This is a no-win situation. I have never seen this work out, unless you like getting fucked up the ass on a regular basis, because that is what is going to happen. See, you are a partner and you own half of nothing, which, by the way, is still nothing. Actually, it's worth less than nothing, but let's not waste time on the details, because they sure won't.

You will be kept completely in the dark about every deal, until it's time to do the labor (which is your job). It's time to get paid, so here comes the family feud! See, your new best friend and partner just got you to do full-time production for part-time money.

Compilation CD Demo

Next on the menu is one of my all-time favorite scams. This particular flim-flam I am quite familiar with, so I know it works. I have been on both the giving and receiving end of this industry mistruth.

In the late '80s, record labels started downsizing and consolidating into smaller, more efficient entities. After all the merging and disman-tlement was over, the industry was left with a lot of little boutique or mom-and-pop labels. This was when someone got smart and decided that it would be easier to shop multiple artists on one CD, in the form of a compilation, than it would be to shop them individually. Hence the birth of the compilation CD demo. This so-called compilation was designed to take as many as twelve different artists and record them on that one CD, which would be distributed amongst the industry, for max-imum exposure with minimum effort.

Here's the catch. You had to break open your piggy bank and get out some loot if you wanted a spot on the almighty compilation album.

If you think about it, it was really an awesome concept, especially if you were a struggling artist or producer looking to gain industry expo-sure. We have all been down that road a time or two, running from one industry function to the next, trying to walk the walk and talk the talk with the members of the elite inner sanctum of the music business, des-perately hoping to cop the right business card or get an opportunity to drop off a demo at a label.

For whatever reason, though, nothing ever comes of the many attempts to get a foot in the door. All hope is lost. Then suddenly, out of nowhere, you get an offer to appear on a compilation album from some elite industry person you probably never heard of before. But it doesn't matter, because all you want is your day in the sun. A group of alleged industry bigwigs are putting together a compilation album featuring your area's hottest new talent. It's the ultimate chance to be exposed nationally, to all the top A&R people in the business. They promise that you will stand out from the droves of other artists seeking a chance at superstardom. Sure, there's a hefty fee, but this is an opportunity of a lifetime! You're not going to miss your chance at fame or fortune.

So after you beg, borrow, and steal every dime you can possibly get your hands on, you send them your demo, along with a signed copy of an exclusive publishing agreement that locks you down like a slave. In return, they send you a few copies of the project CD and a list of the fifty or more record label A&R people who will be personally listening to your material.

Now, six months or more have passed by and there has been not so much as a word from the labels. You decide to call the office of the company who created the CD. The secretary blows more smoke up your ass about being patient, then offers you a chance to secure a spot on their next CD project.

At this point you realize that you have been hoodwinked, bamboozled, and taken advantage of. Firstly, whatever fee they charged you to be part of the album was entirely too much because it doesn't take much money to master and manufacture a few CDs. Secondly, the company claims to have sent out countless CD demos to labels and A&R departments, but there is no way to prove that they actually did mail them out, or even whether they have these contacts they boast about. Finally, you have to figure that since they charged you about $1,000 to be included on the project, and there are a total of twelve artists on the CD, they made about $12,000. It probably cost them $2,000.00 to master and manufacture the CD, so they made about $10,000 off all these unsuspecting artists. In fact, what they probably did was press up enough CDs to send to the artists for their approval and then pocketed the rest of the loot.

The world is a screwed up place, full of plenty of con-artist, scammers, and double-dealers who just want to fuck you out of your hard earned cash. Don't be fooled into thinking that the music business is any different. Rule of thumb, all that glitters isn't gold, it just well may be shit in a gold package.

10

WHAT THE A&R DOESN'T WANT YOU TO KNOW

Okay, pimpin'. It's time we set this shit straight once and for all. There are a lot of different ideas circulating about what A&R people do and what their actual job is. By definition, the term "A&R" stands for Artist and Repertoire. What it means in plain English leaves a lot to the imagination. Usually, it means that you have to deal with a frustrated former artist who is on his own dick because the record company says he is the man with the golden ears. In my experience, the A&R guy is the one that makes the deal happen, but at the same time he's the one who usually gets in the way of the creative flow.

As I mentioned earlier, the A&R is usually someone who had big dreams of becoming a performer him- or herself, but didn't quite cut the muster for whatever reason. Or they might be ex-DJs or managers, or even sometimes the cousin of somebody in a position of power at the company. Regardless of how they were appointed to their station, they are in charge and they will never let you forget it.

The Role of A&R

About a million years ago, the A&R was the person who actually produced the record, and that is why some of them think that it's still part of the job description. I don't want to completely player-hate these people, because for a small period of time I held that same position. A lot of these cats prove to be a necessary evil in the long run, especially when you are an up-and-coming record producer. But like anything else in life, you have the good, the bad, and the ugly. On any given night you can find them in the back of some old, smoky nightclub, listening for the next big act to roll across the stage. Believe me, if you are working the club scenes and open mic nights, you will find them there, lingering in the cigarette smoke. If your shit is the bomb, then believe in the fact that they will seek you out. Like hungry sharks, they will close in on you, ready to strike at a moment's notice. Bam! "Here's my card; call me on Monday at about 1p.m." Why 1p.m., you ask? Oh, I forgot to mention that these muthafuckas are special and they don't get into the office until about noon, then spend their days at meetings and expensive lunches. Not bad, huh?

I have to give them some credit because they are the face of the record company, and it's a stressful-ass job. Most of these cats have an employment cycle of about two years or less, mainly because they are the company's scapegoat. If some shit goes wrong with a project, it's blamed on the A&R. Also, they are on the lower end of the food chain as far as record-company personnel go. So if they work under someone else who gets fired because they aren't performing, well, guess who gets fired along with them. In fact, I have known a record-company president to get fired and his entire department be given the boot right along with him. What can be said about the snowball effect, except that shit flows downhill? I know firsthand, because that's how my short A&R career ended.

An A&R person serves as the liaison between the artist and the label. Though a lot of them have a hidden agenda, they are primarily trying to get the artist signed. Remember, if the A&R does not deliver talent faster than a Domino's Pizza boy, his ass is out of there. This is why A&R people are under so much pressure to sift through the seemingly endless piles of demo tapes that swamp their offices each day. If you think about it, there is no way in hell that they are able to listen to each of the demos that they receive on a daily basis, so if your shit isn't wrapped in a gold package, you better hang that up, homie. It's like winning the lottery. For this very reason, a smart A&R has an assistant and at least two interns to whom they can farm out the listening process.

This can be quite dangerous, depending on the way the A&R treats his people. Record company jobs are performance-based, and the next man is always lurking in the shadows, waiting to take your spot. The opposite to this is that if you have a strong team, which is familiar with your likes and dislikes, a masterpiece can be discovered among the piles of demos.

Record Label Hijinx

In my case, I got my first major record deal because of an overly ambitious intern. This intern would take cassettes that were submitted to the A&R department and bulk erase them in order to reuse them to record his own demos. In fact, if the demo tape was a high-quality cassette, then your demo was as good as erased. It must have been fate, because it just so happened that he got his hands on my tape. He thought he had erased my demo tape and recorded his own material on it, but he was in for a big surprise.

One day he was playing the tape on the system in the A&R's office, when, smack-dab in the middle of his shit, my song came on. Thrown off track by this change in the beat, the A&R put down the phone and asked him, "What the fuck was that?" They played my song several times and realized that they both liked what they heard. The intern was so accustomed to erasing tapes en masse that he hadn't even bothered taking my name off the cassette label. Plus, as a backup, I always record my name and phone number at the end of each song, in anticipation of fucked-up events like these. Impressed by what he had heard, the A&R guy had his secretary get my information off the tape and give me a call. The rest was history.

As anyone can see, shady practices start at the top and drizzle down like acid rain to the assistants and interns below. You have to be on the lookout for some of these guys, because everything isn't always everything. I thought this cat was cool because he gave me my first major deal, but in the end I realized that he was a shark just trying to eat, like everyone else in the game. As time went by, I got to witness his many scams and mistruths for myself. In fact, this A&R guy tried to buy the publishing rights from each producer on a project before the album came out. Look, I'm not claiming to have uncovered a conspiracy, but every producer who sold their share of the publishing had their record dropped as a single from the album; every one of them except me. I held out. I weathered the storm. I did get paid; it took a while, but I got mine. Hold your ground and turn your focus away from the fast buck. These shady characters are out there, just waiting to screw you over if you let them.

The Fabulous Five

Since the dawn of the new millennium, there have been some major changes in the music industry, especially with the use of the Internet and the power of file sharing. Because of all types of corporate mergers and important shit like that, the world is left with only five major recording and distribution companies. They have been called all types of catchy names, but I like to refer to them as the Fabulous Five. They are, in no particular order, Sony Music Entertainment, Universal Music Group (UMG), Bertelsmann Music Group (BMG), Warner Elektra Atlantic (WEA), and CEMA/UNI Distribution.

In some way or another, these five giants are connected to nearly every sub or independent label (there are far too many to list) in the entire world. Needless to say, if you get a record deal on this planet, you are indirectly connected to one of these five majors.

In the past ten years or so, the game has changed dramatically. Labels used to be interested in developing new talent. This is a process where a new act is broken and a small following is created by consecutively dropping albums and building on the previous fan base. By around the time they drop their third album, the artist has become a megastar and sold a million or more records.

These days, though, the whole concept of artist development is out the door. These labels want instant success, right out the box. Just add water and bam, a million-plus the first week it hits the stores. Record companies are no longer concerned with development, only short-term success. Who's got time to develop an artist, especially with all the corporate downsizing and hostile takeovers?

This means that the job of artist development has been left up to the producer or production company. When you're dealing with the Fab Five, your shit better sell at least ten million or you're dead in the water, buddy. Their major concern is developing a worldwide marketing machine, capable of being exploited in every form of media, from the phonograph to the video game. The name of this game is endorsements and corporate sponsorship, so all that old-school Motown total artist development shit has died and long since been buried.

Anyone who was lucky enough to get signed to a major deal before the Fab Five got a brand new attitude would have found themselves suddenly stuck like chuck, with no support, or just plain up shit creek. Nobody is doing you a favor by keeping you on a roster where you are, an artist who will become a tax write-off at the end of the fiscal year. Run, run like a slave in the heat of the southern sun and get the fuck out of that deal any way you can. If you are talented enough and you got a set of balls, you will eventually get another record deal. Consider this: If you get off a major label and get re-signed to a small label, you will still somehow be connected to the Fab Five. But this time you won't have to break out the M.C. Hammer pants and sing songs that sound like Britney Spears, just so you can eat.

A deal with the right sub or independent label can turn out to be just as suitable financially as a direct deal with the Fab Five. In other words, a muthafucka can still get broke off without selling his ass out. Murder Inc. did it, Roc-A-Fella did it, and Aftermath did it. So there is still hope for you. Keep this shit on the low, though, because these are the things that you ain't supposed to know. Artists are stupid and uniformed. Or are they?

Afterthoughts

Never invite the A&R to your session. He will try to involve himself in your project. Fuck that. You need all of your money in your pockets, not his.

Don't listen to any record executive if he says that you need to change your style to sound more like anybody who is currently playing on the radio. Imitation is not a form of flattery, especially in the music business.

Always keep your level of professionalism when dealing with these assholes, regardless of how comfortable they want to get around you. As soon as you let your guard down, you will be violated.

Don't let anyone tell you that things are on a need-to-know basis, or that an artist should only be concerned with the creative portion of a project.

This is the only formula you need to know:

SKILLS + KNOWLEDGE + HARD WORK = SUCCESS

11

PUBLISHING 101

In this hip-hop manual we have covered a lot of the keys to success, but none are as important as the knowledge I am about to drop on you about publishing. This chapter deals with the topic of writing songs, and the relationship between you as a writer and a third-party publisher and/or performing-rights societies.

But before we dive in headfirst, I need to holler at you for a minute about what this shit actually is, and how it can affect your career. Simply put, publishing is money that is made as a result of your songs being played on the radio, or commercially exploited through performance. Publishing income derived from the songs you have written is paid to you in two forms. One is mechanical royalty, and the other is public performance income. You're probably thinking to yourself, "Hey, I'm not a songwriter, I'm a producer. How does publishing affect me?" Well, as a producer You are the main creative force behind any song: you made the track, created the vibe, and probably came up with the hook or concept of the song, too. Well, then that entitles you to a piece of the copyright, and most certainly a piece of the publishing income.

Now that we have established that you are a hip-hop writer as well as a producer, it's time we break down this topic into small pieces that are easy to digest.

The Roles of Songwriters and Publishers

The songwriters write the songs the whole world sings. And if the world is singing your song, that means you are getting lots of airplay. Lots of airplay means lots of publishing royalties. This is the main reason why a writer should start his own publishing company, or enter into a form of agreement with a third-party publishing company.

The music publisher is the business entity that owns or controls the musical compositions and the copyrights of the song. A lot of songwriters serve as their own publishers and therefore own and control their own copyrights. The one who controls the copyright controls the money. Some other writers assign all or a part of the control of their songs to third-party publishing companies. That said, I can't stress enough how important it is to start your own company. But if you do not feel comfortable about handling your own business, hook up with the pros.

Now there is plenty of speculation about what a publisher actually does for a writer/co-publisher, but here is a basic idea.

Advances

If you decide not to go the do-it-yourself route and you hook up with an established publisher, you will probably receive a cash advance for a piece of the publishing income. But before you go out and spend it all, remember that the shit is recoupable. We talked about recoupable money in earlier chapters, so you know what to do.

Licensing

Your publisher will issue mechanical licenses to record companies and sync (synchronization) licenses to companies that want to use your songs. This is why you hear popular songs in movies, videos, games, karaoke, television shows, and commercials. If your songs are really successful, you will find that they've been printed as songbooks and sheet music. You better hope like hell your song gets on a TV show or movie soundtrack, because I know firsthand that the money from those is off the chain. I have had the luxury of both, and believe me, those checks were flowing like Evian.

Collection

It is the responsibility of the publisher to collect the income produced from the licensing of your songs. Once this tedious task has been completed, they then pay the writer (which is you) and the co-publisher (which hopefully is you, if you're not scared to self-publish) their shares of the money, on a quarterly or semi-annual basis.

Pushing Your Song

The publishing company has a team of salespeople whose only job is to promote your songs and get them covered by other artists. They also pitch your songs to advertising companies, TV and movie personnel, as well as videogame manufacturers to use in their products. This means big bucks for you, because in order to use your songs they must obtain a synchronization license from your publisher.

Copyright Registration

It's the publisher's job to register your songs with the U.S. Copyright Office. This is mad important, because your publisher can't go after all of the people who steal your shit unless your work is registered. Also, a good publishing company is always on the lookout for biters.

Career Development

A lot of publishing companies like to hook up their artists and writers with deals with producers and artists who are better established, in order to guide and develop a new artist's career.

The Five Biggest Publishing Companies on the Planet
BMG Music Publishing
Disney Music Publishing
EMI Music Publishing
MCA/PolyGram Music Publishing
Warner/Chappell Music Publishing

Music Publishing Income (Publisher's Share and Writer's Share)

There is a lot of loot to be made in music publishing. If you don't understand how the money gets cut up, you will be left banging your head against the wall. In order to understand what is really going on, you have to understand the difference between the publisher's share and the writer's share of the money. The publisher's share is the part of the money that goes to the owner of the copyright. In some cases, if you have started your own publishing company and entered into a co-publishing agreement with a bigger publishing company, then you will split the fifty percent that is due to the publisher equally, 25/25. If you have not entered into such an agreement, then the publisher's share is half of the total income for the licensing of your songs, which is fifty percent. Because the publisher's share is only half the income, as the writer you're entitled to the other fifty percent of the income from your songs. Of course, that is only if you wrote the song yourself, or you had help from your friends.

The Recap
One-hundred percent publishing share
Fifty percent publisher's share
Fifty percent writer's share
The publisher collects money on the writer's behalf and also handles the administration of the song's copyright.

Helpful Notes
Because copyright laws are a little sketchy concerning hip-hop songs, it's a good idea to share in the copyright of the song with the artist right from the jump, so you don't get fucked out of the deal.

Sources of Income
The four main ways that money is made from music publishing are through mechanical royalties, public performance royalties, synchronization licenses, and print material.

Mechanical Royalties
"Mechanical royalties" refer to money paid by the record company to the publishers of songs that have been "mechanically reproduced" on record or CD. Since this is the biggest way for both the publisher and the writer to get paid, I cannot stress how important it is that the producer co-writes the songs with the artist.

Public Performance Income

The exclusive right of public performance is better known as the performing right. What this means to you, the layperson, is that it allows third parties to publicly perform your songs. Public performances include TV, radio, cable broadcast, bars, nightclubs, and any business that plays music in the background. These entities need to obtain the proper licenses for usage of your material.

No publishing company has time to harass all of these public entities for your money, and therefore they enter into an agreement with a performing rights society that collects the money on the publisher's behalf.

Performing rights societies such as BMI, ASCAP, and SESAC collect this income on the artist's behalf. They offer a blanket license that allows the holder to publicly perform all of the songs in the society's catalog. They also make an attempt to calculate how many times a song is being played during a certain block of time, and then pay both the publisher and the writer their equal shares. The bottom line is that if you want to get paid, you need to hook up with one of the performing rights societies.

For further information on membership, go to:
www.ASCAP.com
www.BMI.com
www.SESAC.com

Okay playa, you're now in the home stretch. It's almost time to get fitted for your cap and gown, but don't start the party just yet. You have just completed one of the most difficult chapters in this book to understand. If you are standing there scratching your head, then I suggest that you read it again and again until it starts to make sense. I have merely scratched the surface on the subject of publishing and there is a lot more information available on the topic if you want to further your skills. Remember, publishing is another way for you to earn income in the music business, and if money doesn't motivate you to learn then nothing ever will.

12

CLOSURE

When I first decided to write this book, I was a little apprehensive. I was worried about whether people would understand where I was coming from. I wondered if what I had to say could serve as a tool to help new artists and producers get on the road to success.

In actuality, this book is an excellent source of information and entertainment for anyone who is looking for a brief explanation of the mechanics of the record business. As I have gotten out there and politicked with the masses, I have noticed the many similarities between people who are breaking into the game. Everyone I have spoken to has spent many sleepless nights and countless dollars in search of the secrets to success in the music business. We have all made sacrifices in pursuit of our dreams. Shit, I can definitely understand what sacrifices are all about, because I have walked in those same shoes. We all make a commitment to succeed, but often find that our attempts are in vain.

The bottom line is that there is no secret key to success in the music business. The sooner you come to terms with that, the better off you will be. Instead of wasting precious time on uncovering the secrets of success, you should spend your time investing in your own talents and skills by enhancing your creativity through practice. There are a million and one ways to skin a cat, and about a billion and one ways to break into the business. The major problem new artists face in this business is that they are not willing to compromise or get past their incredibly large egos enough to see what is going on. Most artists are extremely creative beings and possess a multitude of other talents concerning the arts. They fail to realize that both writing and producing are great tools to help them launch their careers as recording artists. The road to success in any business is usually tough terrain, and the music business is no different. But if an artist takes the time and puts in the energy to lay out a map or virtual blueprint for success, he or she will find that the distance between the bottom rung of the ladder and the top is a lot smaller than could ever be imagined.

Everyone had to start at the bottom rung, and you are no different. I told you earlier that Puff Daddy was an intern at Uptown Records, under Andre Harrell, and look where he ended up. Tupac was a back-up dancer for Digital Underground before he became a rap legend. Keith Sweat was a stockbroker on Wall Street, and both Faith Evans and Ashanti wrote songs for other artists before they got their day in the sun. The proof is definitely in the pudding. What more motivation do you need to get off the couch and get it popping? There are a lot of jobs that make up the behind-the-scenes operations of the music business. Get in where you fit in, and best of luck. You're going to need it.

13

HIP-HOP RESOURCES

*D*isclaimer

The information contained in this section was accurate at press time. Remember that the music business changes fast and not all of these resources may be current by the time you read this book. Always double-check contact names before sending your material.

Audio Recording, Sampling, and Virtual Synths Programs

When outfitting your studio, there are tons of programs that may fit your production style. Here are a few of the most popular options.

Steinberg Cubase SX 3.0-MAC/PC
Bias Deck 3.5-PC
Propellerheads Reason 2.5-MAC/PC
Propellerheads Recycle-MAC/PC
Digidesign Pro Tools LE-MAC/PC
Ableton Live 3.0 Mac/PC
Cakewalk Sonar 3 Producer Edition-PC Only

Cakewalk Project Five-PC Only
Sony Sound Forge 7.0-PC Only
MOTU Digital Performer-MAC Only
MOTU Mach Five Universal Sampler-MAC/PC
Emagic Logic Platinum 6-MAC Only
Native Instruments Kontakt Virtual Sampler-MAC/PC

Suggested Sample Library

Having been a DJ for over twenty years, I have compiled a list of songs that are excellent to use for sampling break beats, hooks, and bass lines. Many artist and producers have used these same songs in whole or part to make some of the hottest hip-hop songs of the past two decades. With a little imagination, you can create all-new hits for the next two decades to enjoy.

Dexter Wansel—"New Beginnings"

24 Carat Black—"Ghetto"

Linda Crawford—"Never Gonna Stop"

George Benson—"Octane"

Jerry Butler—"Never Gonna Give You Up"

Gentle Rain—"Lonely Jelly"

Marlena Shaw—"California Soul"

Art Farmer—"Soul Sides"

James Mtume—"Beyond Forever"

Mighty Tom Cats—"Soul Makossa"

Malcolm McLaren—"World Famous"

Jazz Crusaders—"Studwood"

Luchi De Jesus—"Round Midnight"

Vicki Anderson—"The Land of Milk and Honey"

Monty Alexander—"Love and Happiness"

Quincy Jones—"Up Against the Wall"

24 Carat Black—"Synopsis 2 Mothers' Day"

Monty Alexander—"Love Has a Way"

The Impressions—"On the Move"

The East St. Louis Gospelettes—"Have Mercy On Me"

Dave Grusin—"Either Way"

Billy Paul—"Let's Fall in Love All Over"

Gwen and George McCrae—"The Rub"

Jose Jose—"Guando Vayas Conmigo"

Roberta Flack and Donny Hathaway—"Baby I Love You"

Al Green—"The Letter"

Al Green—"Something"

Henry Mancini—"Theme for the Losers"

Brother Jack McDuff—"Hold it for a Minute"

Minnie Ripperton—"Only When I'm Dreaming"

Gwen McCrae—"It Keeps on Raining"

Rare Earth—"I Know I'm Losing You"

Ruben Wilson—"We're in Love"

Alain Goraguer—"Le Bracelet"

David Axelrod—"The Smile"

Roberta Flack—"Hey, That's No Way to Say Goodbye"

Monty Alexander—"A Time For Love"

Brenda Russell—"A Little Bit of Love"

The Main Ingredient—"Something 'Bout Love"

Survivor—"Eye of the Tiger"

Shawn Phillips—"I Just Came to Say Goodbye"

Chicago Gangsters—"Gangster Boogie"

Ferrante & Teicher—"Christo Redentor"

Bloomfield, Kooper, Stills—"Stop"

Lyn Collins—"Put It on the Line"

Eddie Henderson—"Inside You"

Bobbi Humphrey—"Blacks and Blues"

Al Green—"Gotta Find a New World"

Mulatu of Ethiopia—"Kasalefkut-Hulu"

Hubert Laws—"Modaji"

George Benson—"Changing World"

The Billy Cobham George Duke Band—"Almusta the Beloved"

Hank Carbo—"Hot Pants"

Peter Gennaro—"Hard Knock Life"

Tom Jones—"Ain't No Sunshine"

Nat Adderly—"Rise Sally Rise"

Les McCann—"Roberta"

Joe Williams—"Get Out My Life Woman"

Steve Khan—"Darlin' Darlin' Baby"

Bobbi Humphrey—"San Francisco Lights"

Leon Haywood—"I Want'a Do Something Freaky to You"

Herb Otha—"Living in Dreams"

Les McCann—"Beyond Yesterday"

Kenny Barron—"Sunset"

Chrysalis—"30 Poplar"

The 9th Creation—"Rate of Mind"

Bill Withers—"Kissing My Love"

John Dankworth—"Two Piece Flower"

Glass Prism—"Here You Are"

Johnny Mathis—"Come to Me"

Cannonball Adderly—"Capricorn"

Rare Earth—"Eleanor Rigby"

Lou Donaldson—"It's Your Thing"

Portrait of Petula—"The Windmills of Your Mind"
Minnie Ripperton—"Here We Go"
The Supremes—"It's Time to Break Down"
Alain Goraguer—"Ten Et Tiwa"
Junior Mance—"I Believe to My Soul"
Al Green—"Love and Happiness"
Al Green—"Light My Fire"
Al Green—"Free at Last"
The Moments—"Sexy Mama"
Wendy Rene—"After the Laugh"
Latimore—"Let's Do it in Slow Motion"
The Mad Lads—"Promises of Yesterday"
Herbie Hancock—"Do a Thing"
Eddie Bo—"From This Day On"
Harvey Mason—"Modaji"
Electric Prunes—"Holy Are You"
Hubert Laws—"The Rite of Spring"
The Bubble Gum Machine—"I Wonder"
Billy Joel—"The Stranger"
Quincy Jones—"Rosita"
Cameo—"Hanging Downtown"
Latimore—"Let Me Go"
Main Ingredient—"A Car of Love"
Ray Bryant—"Up above the Rock"
The Outlaws Blues Band—"Deep Guiley"
Melba Moore—"Standing Right Here"
Norman Connors—"The Creator and the Master Plan"
George Benson—"The World is a Ghetto"
Main Ingredient—"Instant Love"
Herb Alpert—"Treasure of San Miguel"
Henry Mancini—"Theme from the Girl from Petrouka"
Idris Muhammad—"Say What"
Brel—"Vieillir"
Lyn Collins—"Take Me Just as I Am"
Larry Mizell—"Shifting Gear"
Melba Moore—"Must Be Dues"
New Birth—"Come On and Dream Some Paradise"
James Brown—"Bring it Up"
Quincy Jones—"Body Heat"
Lowell—"Mellow Mellow Right On"
Zulema—"Love to Last Forever"
David Axelrod—"Terri's Tune"
Les McCann—"The Morning Song "
Grady Tate—"I Can Deliver "
Ann Peebles—"I'm Gonna Tear Your Playhouse Down"
Francis Lai—"In Our Shadow"
Sonny Phillips—"Goin' Home"
Main Ingredient—"Looks Like Rain"

Stanley Turrentine—"Hope That We Can Be Together Soon"
Gill Scott Heron—"The Revolution Will Not Be Televised"
Television's Greatest Hits—"Night Court"
Headhunters—"I Remember I Made You Cry"
Sly Johnson—"Could I Be Fallin' In Love"
Ahmad Jamal—"I Love Music"
George Benson—"Footin' It"
Freddie McCoy—"Gimmie Some"
Bill Dogget—"Honky Tonk"
Ohio Players—"Ecstasy"
Al Green—"You Ought to Be With Me"
Little Richard—"The Rill Thing"
Joe Chambers—"Mind Rain"
David Axelrod—"The Warnings"
Gwen McCrae—"I've Got Nothing to Lose but the Blues"
Booker T. & The M.G.s—"Children Don't Get Weary"
Albert King—"I'll Play the Blues For You"
Ohio Players—"What's Going On"
Average White Band—"School Boy Crush"
Ronnie Laws—"Tidal Waves"
Maynard Ferguson—"Mister Mellow"
Oliver Sain—"On The Hill"
Joe Simon—"Drowning in the Sea of Love"
Willie Mitchell—"Groovin' "
David Axelrod—"Schoolboy"
Julie Driscoll—"Light My Fire"
Hubert Laws—"I Had a Dream"
Electric Company—"Sing Song"
Minnie Ripperton—"Inside My Love"
Gwen McCrae—"90% of Me"
Emotions—"If You Think It"
Baby Huey—"Hard Times"
Ester Phillips—"That's Alright With Me"
B.T. Express—"Everything Good to You"
Roy Ayers—"Sensitize"
Quincy Jones—"Kitty with the Bent Frame (Skit)"
The Sons—"Boom Boom Chop (Skit)"
George Benson—"Smokin' Cheeba Cheeba"
Heath Brothers—"Smilin' Billy Pt 2"
O.V. Wright—"Let's Straighten it Out"
Vicki Anderson—"Message From the Soul Sisters"
Clarence Wheeler & The Enforcers—"Hey Jude"
Tower Of Power—"Sparkling in the Sand"
Tom Scott—"Today"
Ahmad Jamal—"Misdemeanor"
Marvin Gaye—"Poor Abbey Walsh"

Ronnie Foster—"Mystic Brew"

Tony Avalon & The Belairs—"Sexy Coffee Pot"

New Birth—"You Are What I Am About"

Roy Ayers—"Painted Desert"

Dave Grusin—"Modaji"

David Porter—"The Masquerade Is Over"

Electric Prunes—"General Confessional"

Donald Byrd—"Wind Parade"

Thom Bell—"Moses Theme"

Bill Conti—"Philadelphia Morning"

New Birth—"Honeybee"

Love Unlimited—"Move Me No Mountain"

Young Holt Unlimited—"Queen of the Nile"

Bobby Caldwell—"What You Won't Do For Love"

Ramp—"Daylight"

Spinners—"I'm Tired of Giving"

Black Ivory—"I Keep Asking Questions"

Ann Peebles—"Straight from the Heart"

Soul Children—"Move Over"

Glenn Jones—"Show Me"

Michael Jackson—"With a Child's Heart"

Cecil Holmes—"Call Me, Come Back Home"

Russ Barnard—"Let the Sunshine In"

Gary Burton—"Las Vegas Tango"

Flaming Embers—"Gotta Get Away"

Diana Ross—"My Hero is a Gun"

Stephanie Mills—"Starlight"

Jerry Butler—"Take the Time to Tell Her"

Gordon Parks—"From Storm to Calm"

Cat Stevens—"Was Dog a Doughnut?"

Les McCann—"Benjamin"

Love Unlimited—"Under the Influence of Love"

Talking Heads—"Once in a Lifetime"

John Handy—"Alvina"

Jerry Butler—"I'm Your Mechanical Man"

Brother To Brother—"Hey, What's That You Say"

Sylvester—"Was it Something I Said"

Weather Report—"Mysterious Traveller"

Dorothy Ashby—"Cause I Need It"

Crusaders—"Whispering Pines"

Donald Byrd—"I Feel Live Loving You Today"

The Sweet Inspirations—"Why Marry"

Kleer—"Intimate Connection"

Cymande—"Dove"

The Dramatics—"In the Rain"

Monk Higgins—"Little Green Apples"

Bill Conti—"Going the Distance"

Eugene McDaniels—"Jagger the Dagger"

Grover Washington, Jr.—"Loran's Dance"

Jimmy Smith—"I'm Gonna Love You" (Skit)

Billy Brooks—"Forty Days"

Donald Byrd—"Think Twice"

The Chamber Brothers—"Funky"

Rotary Connection—"Memory Lane"

Ramp—"Daylight"

Little Feat—"Fool Yourself" (Skit)

Lou Reed—"Walk on the Wild Side"

Lonnie Smith—"Spinning Wheel" (Skit)

Ruben Wilson—"Inner City Blues"

Kool & The Gang—"Electric Frog"

Art Blakey—"A Chant for Bu"

S.O.B.—"Drums" (Skit)

Weather Report—"Young and Fine"

Gary Bartz—"Gentle Smiles (Saxy)"

Chuck Jackson—"I Like Everything about You" (Skit)

Grant Green—"Down Here on the Ground"

Jackie Jackson—"Is it Him or Me?" (Skit)

Minnie Ripperton—"Baby This Love I Have"

Willis Jackson—"Ain't No Sunshine" (Skit)

Sonny Lester—"Green Dolphin Street"

Paul Humphries—"Uncle Willie's Dream"

Brother Jack McDuff—"Oblighetto"

Jimi Hendrix—"Little Miss Lover" (Skit)

Ronnie Foster—"Mystic Brew"

Brethren—"Inside Love" (Skit)

Lee Morgan—"Absolution"

The Whatnauts—"Why Can't People Be Colors Too"

Bill Cosby—"Martin's Funeral"

Brethren—"Inside Love" (Skit)

Michael Urbaniak Group—"Ekim"

Howard Roberts Quartet—"Dirty Old Bossa Nova"

Luther Ingram—"Pity For the Lonely"

Billy Baron—"Communication Is Where it's At"

Funkadelic—"Nappy Dugout"

Freda Payne—"We've Gotta Find a Way" (Skit)

Sly And The Family Stone—"Remember Who You Are"

Les McCann—"North Carolina"

Cannonball Adderley—"Soul Virgo"

Slave—"Son of Slide"

Roy Ayers—"Running Away"

Average White Band—"Love Your Life"

Funkadelic—"Tales of Kidd Funkadelic"

Kool & The Gang—"Soul Vibrations"

Fatback Band—"Wicky Wacky"

Cal Tjader—"Aquarius"

Jack Wilkins—"Red Clay"

Weldon Irvine—"We've Getting' Down"

Charles Earland—"Low Down"

Milt Jackson—"Olinga"

Steve Arrington—"Beddie Bey"

Kool & The Gang—"Who's Gonna Take the Weight"

James Brown—"Just Enough Room For Storage"

Minnie Ripperton—"Inside My Love"

Clyde McPhatter—"Mixed Up Cup" (Skit)

Bola Sete—"Bettina"

Albino Gorilla—"Psychedelic Shack"

Roy Ayers—"I Feel Like Making Love"

David T. Walker—"On Love"

The Cyrkle—"The Visit"

Gary Burton—"I'm Your Pal"

Henry Franklin—"Soft Spirit

The Impressions—"On the Move"

Lou Donaldson—"Turtle Walk"

Eddie Bo—"From This Day On"

King Curtis—"Instant Groove"

O'Donnell Levy—"We've Only Just Begun"

The Three Degrees—"You're the Fool"

Bama—"Ghettos of the Mind"

Freddie McCoy—"Gimme Some"

The Ohio Players—"What's Going On"

Simtec Wylie—"Bootleggin'"

Mongo Santamaria—"Heighty Ho"

Ernie Hines—"Our Generation"

Kool & The Gang—"Chocolate Buttermilk"

The 9th Creation—"Bubble Gum"

Georgie Fame—"Music Talk"

Eugene McDaniels—"Freedom Dance"

Eddy Senay—"Cameo"

Tom Scott—"Today"

Alyn Ainsworth—"Where Do I Go"

The 5 Stair Steps—"Don't Change Your Love"

Backyard Heavies—"Expo 83"

Gentlemen & Ladies—"Party Time"

Cannonball Adderly—"Capricorny"

The Ambassadors—"Ain't Got the Love"

Mel & Tim—"Groovy Situation"

Bama—"I Got Soul"

Judy Foster—"Soul Girl"

Billy Paul—"Let's Fall in Love All over Again"

M.F.S.B.—"Sunnin' and Funnin'"

Barbara Mason—"A Good Man is Gone"

Latimore—"Let's Do it in Slow Motion"

Jeff Beck—"Come Dancing"

Grand Master Flash—"Flash is on the Beat Box"

Paul Horn—"Here's that Rainy Day"

The Supremes—"It's Time to Break Down"

War—"Deliver the Word"

Theme from Dark Shadows"

Les McCann—"Beyond Yesterday"

The Originals—"Fantasy Interlude"

Dizzy Gillespie—"A Night in Tunisia"

JBs—"Bring it Up"

The Pointer Sisters—"Don't Drive Me Crazy"

The Blackbyrds—"Wilford's Gone"

Thunder and Lightning—"Bumpin' Bus Stop"

Fred Wesley—"Four Play"

Marlena Shaw—"California Soul"

The Meters—"Funky Miracle"

Jean-Jacques Perrey—"E.V.A."

Caesar Frazier—"Funk it Down"

Sugar Billy Gardner—"I Got Some"

Melvin Bliss—"Synthetic Substitution"

Brother Soul—"Cookies"

The Grassroots—"You and Love Are the Same"

The Commodores—"Assembly Line"

Kid Dynamite—"Uphill Peace of Mind"

Ester Williams—"Last Night Changed it All"

20th Century Steel Band—"Heaven and Hell Is
    Here on Earth"

Jackson Five—"It's Great to Be Here"

Dexter Wansel—"The Theme from the Planets"

Chi Lites—"Help Wanted"

Suggested Reading

You can never learn too much about the music business. Here are some other books you may want to check out.

Brabec, Jeffrey and Brabec, Jeff. *Music, Money and Success*, New York: Schirmer Trade Books, 2004.

D., Chuck and Jah, Yusef. *Fight the Power: Rap, Race, and Reality*, New York: Delta, 1998.

George, Nelson. *Hip Hop America*, New York: Penguin Books, 1999.

Mitchell, Kevin. *Hip-Hop Rhyming Dictionary*, New York: Alfred Publishing Co., 2003.

Rudsenske, J.S. *Music Business Made Simple: A Guide to Becoming a Recording Artist*, New York: Schirmer Trade Books, 2004.

Shakur, Tupac. *The Rose That Grew From Concrete*, New York: MTV Books, 1999.

McPherson, Brian. *Get It In Writing*, New York: Hal Leonard, 1999.

Greene, Roger. *The 48 Laws Of Power*, New York: Penguin Putnam, 2000.

Passman, Donald. *All You Need To Know About The Music Business*, New York: Simon and Schuster, 2003.

Avalon, Moses. *Confessions of A Record Producer: How to Survive the Scams and Shams of the Music Business*, San Francisco: Backbeat Books, 2002.

Kashif and Greenberg, Gary. *Everything You'd Better Know About the Record Industry*, Venice, CA: Brooklyn Boy Books, 1996.

Johnson, Spencer. *Who Moved My Cheese?*, New York: Putnam, 1998.

A&Rs

This section will hook you up with A&R across the country.

Pop/Urban

James Dowdall

Epic Records

550 Madison Ave., 22nd floor

New York, NY 10022

Tel: 212 833 8000

Fax: 212 833 8216

David McPherson

Epic Records

550 Madison Ave., 22nd Floor

New York, NY 10022

Tel: 212 833 8000

Fax: 212 833 8216

Rosa Noone

Epic Records

550 Madison Ave., 22nd floor

New York, NY 10022

Tel: 212 833 8000

Fax: 212 833 8216

Steve McKeever

Hidden Beach Recording

3030 Nebraska Ave., Penthouse Suite

Santa Monica, CA 90404

Tel: 310 453 1400

Fax: 310 453 6760

Urban

Andre Young

Aftermath Records

2220 Colorado Blvd.

Santa Monica, CA 90404

Tel: 310 865 7642

Fax: 310 865 7068

Sean Combs

Bad Boy Entertainment

1540 Broadway, 33rd floor

New York, NY 10036

Tel: 212 930 7005

Fax: 212 381 1599

Perry Watts-Russell

Capital Records

1750 North Vine St., 10th floor

Hollywood, CA 90028

Tel: 323 462 6552

Fax: 323 469 4542

Brian & Ronald Williams

Cash Money Records

P.O. Box 547

Saint Rose, LA 70087

Tel: 504 466 5115

Fax: 504 466 7575

Kevin Liles, Randy Acker

Def Jam Recordings

825 Eighth Ave., 27th floor

New York, NY 10019-7472

Tel: 212 333 8000

Fax: 212 445 3611

Kevin Lee

Hendu Entertainment

P.O. Box 19379

Atlanta, GA 31126

Tel: 404 524 7944

Fax: 404 524 7945

Steve Stoute

Interscope Records

825 Eighth Avenue

New York, NY 10019

Tel: 212 388 8300

Fax: 212 388 8400

Tina Davis

Island/Def Jam

825 Eighth Ave., 27th floor

New York, NY 10019

Tel: 212 333 8000

Fax: 212 445 3228

Wayne Williams

Jive Records

700 N. Green, Suite 200

Chicago, IL 60622

Tel: 312 942 9700

Fax: 312 942 9800

Matt Life

Loud Records

79 Fifth Ave., 16th floor

New York, NY 10003

Tel: 212 337 5300

Fax: 212 337 5366

Chris Lorenzo & Donnell Nichols

Murder INC.

825 Eighth Ave., 20th floor

New York, NY 10019

Tel: 212 333 1330

Fax: 212 445 3662

Andrew Sahck

Priority Records

6430 Sunset Blvd., Suite 900

Los Angeles, CA 90028

Tel: 323 467 0151

Fax: 323 856 8796

Shawn Carter a.k.a. Jay-Z

Roc-a-Fella Records

825 Eighth Ave., 19th floor

New York, NY 10019

Tel: 212 333 8000

Fax: 212 445 3616

Shivon Dean

Ruff Ryder Entertainment

312 E. 53rd St., Suite 208

New York, NY 10022

Tel: 212 315 9800

Fax: 212 445 0997

Ted Lucas

Slip N Slide Records

99 Miami Gardens Dr., Suite 128

Miami, FL 33169

Tel: 305 770 0771

Fax: 305 770 9959

Bill Walker

Thump Records

3101 Pomona Blvd.

Pomona, CA 91768

Tel: 909 595 2144

Fax: 909 598 7028

Ian Steaman

Tommy Boy Records

902 Broadway,13th floor

New York, NY 10010

Tel: 212 388 8300

Fax: 212 388 8400

Tony Mercedes

Tony Mercedes Records

Fayetteville, GA 30214

Tel: 770 719 2800

Fax: 404 767 0247

Pop/Rock/Dance/ Urban/MoR/Country

Al Teller

Atomic Pop

1447 Cloverfield Blvd., Suite 201

Santa Monica, CA 90404

Tel: 310 309 8600

Fax: 310 309 8601

Michael Taylor

Maverick Records

1290 Avenue of the Americas, 9th floor

New York, NY 10019

Tel: 212 399 6973

Fax: 212 315 5590

College Radio

Send these stations your demo and bio, and with a little luck you may be on your way to stardom.

ACRN
Jon Minch
Athens, OH 99.3 FM
Tel: 740 593 4910
acrn@oak.cats.ohiou.edu

CFBU
Sean McLellan
St. Catherines, ON 103.7 FM
Tel: 905 688 5550
cfbu@niagra.com

CFRC
Peggy Shanks
Kingston, ON 101.9 FM
Tel: 613 533 2121
cfrcfm@post.queen.ca

CFUV
Jason L'Hirondelle
Victoria, BC 101.9 FM
Tel: 250 721 8702
Music@cfuv.uvic.ca

CHRW
Bry Webb
London, ON 101.9 FM
Tel: 519 661 3601
chrwmp@julian.uwo.ca

CHRY
Chris Penrose
North York, ON 105.5 FM
Tel: 416 736 5293
chry@yorku.ca

CHSR
Steve Hodgson
Fredericton, NB 97.9FM
Tel: 506 453 4985
chsrmd@unb.ca

CHYZ
Martin Premont
Quebec City, QC 94.3 FM
Tel: 418 656 2131
chyz@public.ulaval.ca

CIBL
Sylvain Lafreniere
Montreal 101.5 FM
Tel: 514 526 2581

CIUT
Roozbeh Showleh
Toronto, ON 89.5 FM
Tel: 416 978 0909
r-burd@ciut.fm

CJAM
Leona Atkins
Detroit, MI 91.5 FM
Tel: 519 971 3606
gagnies@uwindsor.ca

CJSF
Matt Chan
Burnaby, BC 93.9 FM
Tel: 604 291 3076
cjswfm@ucalgary.ca

CKCU
Jennifer Tattersall
Ottawa, ON 93.1 FM
Tel: 613 520 2898
ckuc@web.net

CKUT
Azar S.
Montreal, PQ 90.3 FM
Tel: 514 398 6787
music@ckut.ca

KAFA
D.J. Red
USAF Academy, CO 104.3 FM
Tel: 719 333 4644

KBGA
Ryan Michie
Missoula, MT 89.9 FM
Tel: 406 243 5715

KBUT
Alex Fenion
Crested Butte, CO 90.3 FM
Tel: 970 349 5225
Music@kbut.org

KBUX
Harmeet Kala
Columbus, OH 91.1 FM
Tel: 614 292 0436
radio@underground.fm

KCFV
Torrey Davis
St. Louis, MO 89.5 FM
Tel: 314 595 4463

KCMU
Mr. Supreme
Seattle, WA 90.3 FM
Tel: 206 543 3685

KCSB
Matt Kawamura
Santa Barbara, CA 91.9 FM
Tel: 805 893 3757

KDVS
Rav Sidhu
Davis, CA 90.3 FM
Tel: 530 752 9903
Musicdept@kdvs.org

KFJC
Ken Hamilton
Los Altos Hills, CA 89.7 FM
Tel: 650 949 7092
musicdept@kfjc.org

KFLI
Kurt Liedtke
Prescott, AZ FM
Tel: 520 708 3785
kfli@pr.erau.edu

KGLT
Eammon Bryers
Bozeman, MT 91.9 FM
Tel: 406 994 6483
kgltmus@montana.edu

KJHK
Kareem
Lawrence, KS 90.7 FM
Tel: 785 864 5483
kjhkreq@raven.cc.unkans.edu

KMSA
Isaiah Seabery
Grand Junction, CO 91.3 FM
Tel: 970 248 1718
kmsa@mesastate.edu

KNWD
Bobby Hemsell
Natchitoches, LA 91.7 FM
Tel: 318 357 4180
knwd@alpha.nsula.edu/knwd

KOFA
Greg Bridges
Berkeley, CA 94.1 FM
Tel: 510 848 6767

KPHS
Jonathan Lyons
Pasadena, CA CaFM
Tel: 626 798 8901

KRNL
Darius Alexander
Mt. Vernon, IA 89.7 FM
Tel: 319 895 4431
krnl@cornell-iowa.edu

KRUX
Domskiluv
Las Cruces, NM 91.5 FM
Tel: 505 646 4640
krux@nmsu.edu

KSBR
Tomis Minter
Mission Viejo, CA 88.5 FM
Tel: 949 582 4983

KSCU
Bobby Torres
Santa Carla, CA 103.3 FM
Tel: 408 554 4907

KSHU
Chris Chernoch
Huntsville, TX 90.5 FM
Tel: 936 294 1344
Rtf-kshu@shsu.edu

KSUA
Ryan Sollee
Fairbanks, AK 91.5 FM
Tel: 907 474 7054

KTAO
Peter Merscher
Taos, NM 101.9 FM
Tel: 505 758 5826
dub@spaceplace.com

KTRU
DL
Houston, TX 91.7 FM
Tel: 713 348 4098
noise@ktru.org

KTUH
Kavet Omo
Honolulu, HI 90.3 FM
Tel: 808 348 4098

KUNM
Leo Dexter
Albuquerque, NM 89.9 FM
Tel: 505 277 8022
kunmmus@unm.edu

KUOM
Aaron Szopinski
Minneapolis, MN 770 AM
Tel: 612 625 3500
Music@radioK.org

KUWS
Corey Hallston
Superior, WI 91.3 FM
Tel: 715 394 8530
kuws@iname.com

KVRX
Les Jacobs
Austin, TX 91.7 FM
Tel: 512 232 5431

KVSC
Matt Moeller
St. Cloud, MN 88.1 FM
Tel: 320 255 3126
music@kvsc.org

KWSB
Frank Jackson
Gunnison, CO 91.1 FM
Tel: 970 943 3033

KWTS
J. Cloyd
Canyon, TX 91.1 FM
Tel: 806 651 2797
kwts@mail.wtamu.edu

KWVA
Gene Chism
Eugene, OR 88.1 FM
Tel: 541 345 4091
kwva@gladstone.uoregon.edu

KZSC
Eric Olsen
Santa Cruz, CA 88.1 FM
Tel: 831 459 2811

KZSU
Mike McDowell
Sanford, CA 90.1 FM
Tel: 650 723 4839
music@kzsu.sanford.edu

KZUU
Ian Golash
Pullman, WA 90.7 FM
Tel: 509 335 2208
Kzuu@wsa.edu

Music Choice
Damon Williams
West Orange, NJ cable FM
Tel: 973 731 0500
aneiman@musicchoice.com

WAIH
Seth Warren
Potsdam, NY 90.3 FM
Tel: 315 267 4888
waih@potsman.edu

WARC
Chuck Buseck
Meadville, PA 90.3 FM
Tel: 814 332 3376

WBUQ
Matt Temchatin
Bloomsburg, PA
91.1 FM
Tel: 570 389 4686
wbuq@planetx.bloomu.edu

WBWC
John Elmo
Berea, OH 88.3 FM
Tel: 440 826 2145
wbwc@bw.edu

WBZC
Will Chill
Pemberton, NJ 88.9 FM
Tel: 609 894 9311

WCBN
Chill Will
Ann Arbor, MI 88.3 FM
Tel: 734 763 3500
music@wcbn.org

WCCR-4
RUTGERS University
Pat Wallace
Camden, NJ CC
Tel: 609 225 6168

WCUR
Drew Cochram
West Chester, PA 99.7 FM
Tel: 610 436 2414
wcur@wcupa.edu

WCWS
Ravi Rai
Wooster, OH 90.9 FM
Tel: 330 263 2240
wcws@acs.wooster.edu

WDBK
Chris B.
Blackwood, NJ 91.5 FM
Tel: 609 227 7200

WDBM
Rich Stannard
East Lansing, MI 88.9
Tel: 517 353 4414
Wdbm89fm@pilot.msu.edu

WDCE
Steve E.
Richmond, VA 90.1 FM
Tel: 804 289 8698
wdce@richmon.edu

WDJM
Eric Oglesby
Framingham, MA
91.3 FM
Tel: 508 626 4623

WDPS
Mike Reisz
Dayton, OH 89.5 FM
Tel: 937 542 7182

WDTU
Big Mike
Delhi, NY 107.9 FM
Tel: 607 746 4380

WDWN
Da Spanish
Auburn, NY 89.1 FM
Tel: 315 255 1743
wdwn@hotmail.com

WECB
Bernardo
Boston, MA 98.9 CaFM
Tel: 617 824 8850
wecbmusic@hotmail.com

WECS
Johnny Sample
Willimantic, CT 90.1 FM
Tel: 860 465 5354
wecs@hotmail.com

WEFT
Don Bishop
Champaign, IL 90.1 FM
Tel: 217 581 7370

WERG
Tom Duska
Erie, PA 89.9 FM
Tel: 814 871 5841
werg@gannon.edu

WESS
Mark "Blizzurd" Weber
E. Stroudsburg, PA 90.3
Tel: 570 422 3099
wessfm@hotmail.com

WFIT
Kris Miller
New York, NY 540 AM
Tel: 212 217 7798
wfit@yahoo.com

WFMU
Brain Turner
Jersey City, NJ
91.1 FM
Tel: 201 521 1416

WFNM
Pesci
Lancaster, PA 89.1 FM
Tel: 717 291 4098
wfam-radio@acad.fandm.edu

WGCC
Brian Hillabush
Batavia, NY 90.7 FM
Tel: 716 343 0055
Wgcc@sunygenesee.cc.ny.us

WGTB
Brendan Kredell
Washington, DC 92.3 FM
Tel: 202 687 3702
wgtb@gusun.georgetown.edu

WHCS
590 AM
Tel: 212 772 4276

WHFR
Andre "Face" Reese
Dearborn, MI 89.0 FM
Tel: 313 845 9783
whrf-md@hfcc.net

WHUS
Anthony Tran
Storrs, CT 91.7 FM
Tel: 860 486 4007
whusfm@yahoo.com

WIDR
Brandon McClain
Kalamazoo, MI 89.1 FM
Tel: 616 387 6306

WIXQ
Will "DJ Steez" Smith
Millersville, PA
91.7 FM
Tel: 717 872 3333
ghotirock@aol.com

WKPS
Nate Abney
State College, PA 90.7 FM
Tel: 814 865 7983
polyethylene@psu.edu

WLCA
Jason Kaul
Godfrey, IL 89.9 FM
Tel: 618 466 8936
wlca@ic.cc.il.us

WLIU
Paul Cassella
South Hampton, NY
Tel: 516 287 8289

WLSO
Lam Nguyen
Sault Ste. Marie, MI 90.1FM
Tel: 906 635 2107
wlso@lakers/ssu.edu

WMFO
Susruta Misra/Dan
Medford, MA 91.5 FM
Tel: 617 625 0800
wmfomusic@yahoo.com

WMHW
Aaron K.
Mt. Pleasant, MI 91.5 FM
Tel: 517 774 7287

WMTU
Lady Ace
Houghton, MI 91.9 FM
Tel: 906 487 2333

WNMC
Mike King
Traverse City, MI FM
Tel: 616 922 1091
wnmc@lnmc.edu

WNRN
Rodney Steepe
Charlottesville, VA 91.9 FM
Tel: 804 971 4096
meffle@hotmail.com

WNTE
Jason Feather
Mansfield, PA 89.5 FM
Tel: 570 662 4652
wnte@wheat.mnsfld.edu

WONY
David Castellano
Oneonta, NY 90.9 FM
Tel: 607 436 2712

WOUI
J.D.
Chicago, IL 88.9 FM
Tel: 312 567 3087

WOWL
Vincent Williams
Boca Raton, FL 91.7 FM
Tel: 561 297 3759

WPHS
Derek Genereaux
Warren, MI 89.1 FM
Tel: 810 574 3137
wphs@nevaeh.com

WPSC
Tre
Wayne, NJ 88.7 FM
Tel: 973 720 2448

WPTS
Brandon Glova
Pittsburgh, PA 92.1 FM
Tel: 412 648 7992
wpts@pitt.edu

WQFS
Wesley Elam
Greensboro, NC
90.9 FM
Tel: 336 316 2352

WQMC
Nick Diunte
Flushing, NY
Tel: 718 997 3896

WRBB
Jose Masso
Boston, MA 104.9 FM
Tel: 617 373 4339
wrbb-gm@lynx.neu.edu

WRCU
Tracey Todd
Hamilton, NY 90.1 FM
Tel: 315 228 7104

WRFL
Shareef Abdullah
Lexington, KY 88.1 FM
Tel: 606 257 1557

WRKC
Phil Bendsen
Wilkes-Barre, PA
88.5 FM
Tel: 507 208 5931
wrkc@kings.edu

WRLC
Neftali Flores
Piscataway, NJ
90.3 FM
Tel: 732 445 4105

WRPI
DJ Toast
Troy, NY 91.5 FM
Tel: 518 276 2648
wrpi-md@rpi.edu

WRPW
Jon Benedon
Pleasantville, NY
630 AM
Tel: 914 773 3703
wrpw@stmail.pace.edu

WXYC
Franz
Chapel Hill, NC 89.3 FM
Tel: 919 962 7768
wxyc@unc.edu

Record Labels

You'll need to know who's who when it comes to record labels. Here's the 411.

143 Records
530 Wilshire Blvd., Suite 101
Santa Monica, CA 90401
Tel: 310 899 0143
Fax: 310 899 0133

Aftermath Records
2220 Colorado Blvd.
Santa Monica, CA 90404
Tel: 310 865 7642
Fax: 310 865 7068

Arista Records
6 W. 57th St.
New York, NY 10019

ASCAP
Moe Rodriquez, Regional Rep
P.O. Box 14189
Gainesville, FL 32604
Tel: 352 377 1003
Fax: 352 377 0590
promoe@gator.net

A Touch of Jazz
444 N. Third St.
Philadelphia, PA 19123
Tel: 215 928 9192
Fax: 215 928 9487

Bad Boy Entertainment
1540 Broadway
30th Floor
New York, NY 10036

Blackground Records
101 West 23rd St., Suite 2342
New York, NY 10011

Blackground Entertainment NY
49 West 27th St.
New York, NY 10001
Tel: 212 684 1975
Fax: 212 684 1624

Capital Records
A&R Dept
1750 North Vine & Hollywood
Hollywood, CA 90028
Tel: 323 462 6552

Cash Money Records
P.O. Box 547
St. Rose, LA 70087
Tel: 504 466 5115
Fax: 504 466 7575

Chrysalis Music
Valerie L. Patton
8500 Melrose Ave., Suite 207
Los Angeles, CA 90069-5145
Tel: 310 967 0303
Fax: 310 652 2024

Darkchild Entertainment
503 Doughty Rd.
Pleasantville, NJ 08232
Tel: 609 652 7906
Fax: 609 407 0596

DAS Communications
83 Riverside Dr.
New York, NY 10024
Tel: 212 877 0400
Fax: 212 595 0176

Ebony Son Management
c/o Chaka Zulu
1867 7th Ave., Suite 4C
New York, NY 10026
Tel: 917 449 2619
Fax: 212 665 9634
jdixon914@aol.com

EMI Music Publishing NY
c/o Paul Morgan
1290 Avenue of the Americas
New York, NY 10104
Tel: 212 492 1200
Fax: 212 492 1865
pmorgan@emimusicpub.com

First String Entertainment
Kenny Goodin
Tel: 305 571 8568

Flyte Tyme Productions
4100 West 76th St.
St. Edina, MN 55435
Tel: 612 897 3901
Fax: 612 897 1942
www.flytetyme.com

Freeworld Entertainment
576 A Trabert Ave.
NW Atlanta, GA 30309
Tel: 404 351 6680
Fax: 404 351 1354

Hardball Records
Pablo Casals
350 Lincoln Rd., Suite 316
Miami Beach, FL 33139
Tel: 305 674 7044
Fax: 305 674 7501

Illonize Entertainment Group, Inc.
Disha Crawford
601 S. LaSalle St., Suite D532
Chicago, IL 60605
Tel: 773 250 3029
Fax: 312 777 4000
IllnoizeEnt@aol.com

Interscope Records
10900 Wilshire Blvd., Suite 1230
Los Angeles, CA 90024

Keep Close Entertainment
Tony Rudd
2700 SF Charles Rd
Bellwood, IL 60104
Tel: 708 701 9491
keepclose@html

LaFace Records
Flent Coleman
6 West 57th St.
New York, NY 10019

LaFace Records
3350 Peachtree Rd., Suite 1500
Atlanta, GA 30326
Tel: 404 848 8050
Fax: 404 848 8051

Luke Records
Julian Boothe
Miami, FL
Tel: 305 532 7696

Main Street Records
Danny Browne
Jamaica, WI
Tel: 876 905 1038

McBowman Consulting Group
Michael Bobbit, Royalty Auditing / Publishing
Administration
57 West 38th St., Suite 600
New York, NY 10018
Tel: 212 398 6630
Fax: 212 398 9749
embobbitt@aol.com

Mercury Records
825 Eighth Ave.
New York, NY 10019

Miles Ahead Entertainment
Sheila Eldridge
380 Piermont Ave.
Hillsdale, NJ 07642
Tel: 201 722 1500
Fax: 201 722 1119

Pandisc Music Corp.
Bo Crane
6157 N.W. 167th St., Suite F-11
Miami, FL 33015
Tel: 305 557 1915

Quincy Jones Music
3800 Barham Blvd 503
Los Angeles, CA 90068
Tel: 323 882 1337
Fax: 323 874 4236

Rap-A-Lot Records
P.O. Box 924190
Houston, TX 77292
Tel: 713 335 1600

RJAC Records and Entertainment
Freddie Foxx
P.O. Box 247
Horseshoe Hill Rd.
Pound Ridge, NY 10576

Rockwilder Entertainment
Ellis Entertainment
900 South Ave., Suite 300
Staten Island, NY 10314
Tel: 718 568 3655
Fax: 718 568 3643
ellisentertain@aol.com

Slip-N-Slide Records
Keith Hamilton
99 Miami Gardens Dr., Suite 128
Miami, FL 33169
Tel: 305 770 0771

So So Def Recordings
685 Lambert Dr.
Atlanta, GA 30324
Tel: 404 888 9900
Fax: 404 888 9901

Soundbwoy Entertainment
Lancelot
2221 N.E. 164th, Suite 255
North Miami Beach, FL 33160
Tel: 305 769 9700
Fax: 305 769 6990

Street Street Entertainment
Mark St. Juste
Tel: 310 226 6780

T-Luv Management
3018 Gary Drive
St. Louis, MO 63121
Tel: 314 385 1848
Fax: 314 383 2393

Tommy Boy Records
Ian Stemmans
902 Broadway, 13th floor
New York, NY 10010
Tel: 212 777 0281

Trackmasters Entertainment
550 Madison Ave.
New York, NY 10022
Tel: 212 833 7962
Fax: 212 833 4797

TVT Records
Rell Lefarg
23 East 45th St.
New York, NY 10003
Tel: 212 979 6410

Untouchables Entertainment Group
100 Piermont Rd.
Closter, NJ 07624
Tel: 201 767 6924
Fax: 201 784 3879

Warlock Records, Inc.
126 Fifth Ave., 2nd floor
New York, NY 10011
Tel: 212 206 0800
Fax: 212 206 1949

Warner/Chappell Music
Latin Division
763 Collins Ave., Suite 301
Miami, FL 33139
Tel: 305 534 1010
Fax: 305 534 1082

Wish Recordings
Ian Burke
PMB 145, 541 10th St.
Atlanta, GA 33018
Tel: 404 627 8329

Wright Stuff Records
Donna Wright
P.O. Box 2600
Windmere, LF 34786
Tel: 407 291 8333 ext 1
Fax: 407 291 6946
Voice: 800 222 6000
wrightstuffmanagement.com

Worldwide Entertainment
Kevin Wales
Atlanta, GA
404-760-0599

Zomba / Jive Records
Jimmy Mays
137-139 West 25th St.
New York, NY 10001
Tel: 212 727 0016

Major Record Labels

These are the major players.

A&M Records
1416 North Lebrea Ave.
Hollywood, CA 90028

American Recordings
3500 West Olive Ave.
Suite 1550
Burbank, CA 91505

Angel/Virgin Classics Records
810 Seventh Ave.
New York, NY 10019

Arista Records
6 West 57th Ave.
New York, NY 10019

Atlanta Records
75 Rockefeller Plaza
New York, NY 10019

Blue Note Records
1290 Sixth Ave.
New York, NY 10019

BMG/RCA Records
1540 Broadway, 9th floor
New York, NY 10036

Capitol Records
1750 North Vine St.
Hollywood, CA 90028

Chrysalis Records
1290 Avenue of the Americas
New York, NY 10104

Columbia Records
550 Madison Ave.
New York, NY 10022

East/West Records
75 Rockefeller Plaza
New York, NY 10019

Elektra Records
75 Rockefeller Plaza
New York, NY 10019

EMI Records
1290 Sixth Ave.
New York, NY 10104

Geffen Record Co.
9130 Sunset Blvd., Suite 1230
Los Angeles, CA 90069

Gramophone
P.O. Box 910
Beverly Hills, CA 90213

Interscope Records
10900 Wilshire Blvd., Suite 1230
Los Angeles, CA 90024

Island Records (Polygram)
825 Eighth Ave.
New York, NY 10019

Mammoth Records
101 B St.
Carrboro, NC 27510

Matador Records
676 Broadway
New York, NY 10012

Maverick Music Co.
8000 Beverly Blvd.
Los Angeles, CA 90048

MCA Records
70 Universal City Plaza
University, CA 91608

Mercury Records
825 Eighth Avenue
New York, NY 10019

Motown Records
5750 Wilshire Blvd., Suite 300
Los Angeles, CA 90026

Nonesuch Records
590 Fifth Ave., 16th floor
New York, NY 10036

Polygram Label Group
825 Eighth Ave.
New York, NY 10019

Reprise Records
3300 Warner Blvd.
Burbank, CA 91510

Revolution Records
8900 Wilshire Blvd
Beverly Hills, CA 90211

Rhino Entertainment
10635 Santa Monica Blvd., 2nd floor
Los Angeles, CA 90025

Rounder Records
1 Camp St.
Cambridge, MA 02140

Sire Records
75 Rockefeller Plaza
New York, NY 10019

Verve Records
825 Eighth Ave.
New York, NY 10019

Virgin Records
338 N. Foothill Rd.
Beverly Hills, CA 90210

Warner Bros. Records
3300 Warner Blvd.
Burbank, CA 91505

Windham Hill Records
75 Willow Rd.
Menlo Park, CA 94025

Artist Management

When you're ready, start looking for a manager. There's a list below.

Urban

Luci Raoff
Artistic Control Management USA
685 Lambert Dr.
Atlanta, GA 30324
Tel: 404 733 5511
Fax: 404 733 5512

Ray Copeland
Bar Management
314 W 53rd St., Suite 33
New York, NY 10019
Tel: 212 765 5800
Fax: 212 765 5806

Michele Williams
Big Cat Management
461 Leslie St.
Newark, NJ 07112
Tel: 973 705 3392
Fax: 973 282 0638

Michele Williams
Big Cat Management
461 Leslie St.
Newark, NJ 07112
Tel: 973 705 3392
Fax: 973 282 0638

Ronald Williams
Big Money Management
P.O. Box 547
Saint Rose, LA 70087
Tel: 504 466 5115
Fax: 504 466 7575

Brian Williams
Big Money Management
P.O. Box 547
Saint Rose, LA 70087
Tel: 504 466 5115
Fax: 504 466 7575

Corey Smyth
Blacksmith Management
156 West 56th St.
New York, NY 10019
Tel: 212 586 2112
Fax: 212 586 2116

Kenneth Crear
Creative Management Group USA
3314 Wilshire Blvd.
Los Angeles, CA 90010
Tel: 323 931 7351
Fax: 323931 9251

Dan Dalton
Dan Dalton USA
5765 Hesperia Ave.
Encino, CA 91316
Tel: 818 342 1616
Fax: 818 342 5164

Donna Perillo
DAS Communications USA
83 Riverside Dr.
New York, NY 10024
Tel: 212 877 0400
Fax: 212 595 0176

David Passick
David Passick Entertainment USA
3 E. 28th St., 6th floor
New York, NY 10016
Tel: 212 696 9077
Fax: 212 696 9455

Michael Williams
Family Tree Management
825 Eighth Ave., 20th floor
New York, NY 10019
Tel: 212 445 3316
Fax: 212 445 3500

Michael William
Family Tree Management USA
825 Eighth Ave., 20th floor
New York, NY 10019
Tel: 212 445 3316
Fax: 212 445 3500

Barkue Tubman
Family Tree Management
825 Eighth Ave., 20th floor
New York, NY 10019
Tel: 212 445 3316
Fax: 212 445 3500

Paul Rosenberg
Goliath Artist
270 Lafayette St.
New York, NY 10012
Tel: 212 324 2410
Fax: 212 324 2415

Kedar Massenburg
Kedar Entertainment
1755 Broadway
New York, NY 10019
Tel: 212 373 0750
Fax: 212 489 9096

Jerome Hipps
Mama's Boys Management
7000 Lindberg Blvd., Suite 8001
Philadelphia, PA 19153
Tel: 215 668 7345
Fax: 215 991 9535

Michael McArthur
Mama's Boys Management USA
7000 Lindberg Blvd., Suite 8001
Philadelphia, PA 19153
Tel: 215 668 7345
Fax: 215 991 9535

Marvin McIntyre
Marvelous Enterprises USA
1676 Deefor Cr.
Atlanta, GA 30318
Tel: 404 367 9122
Fax: 404 367 9123

Sheila Eldridge
Miles Ahead Entertainment USA
380 Piermont Ave.
Hillside, NJ 07642
Tel: 201 722 1500
Fax: 201 722 1119

Michelle Le Fleur
ML Entertainment
6709 La Tijera Blvd., Suite 159
Los Angeles, CA 90045
Tel: 323 769 4224
Fax: 310 910 8791

Musa Moore
Moore Flavor Entertainment USA
156 West 56th St., 4th floor
New York, NY 10019
Tel: 718 778 5019
Fax: 718 778 5420

Matthew Knowles
Music World Management USA
9898 Bissonnet St., Suite 625
Houston, TX 77036
Tel: 713 772 5175
Fax: 713 772 3034

Jeffery Rolle
Priceless Music Management USA
2771 Lawrenceville Hwy., Suite 206
Decatur, GA 30033
Tel: 707 724 1933
Fax: 707 724 1987

Hillary Weston
Rock Management/Queen Bee USA
127 West 22nd St., 2nd floor
New York, NY 10011
Tel: 212 414 5930
Fax: 212 414 5934

Jason Jackson
Seven Days Entertainment USA
No public address
New York
Tel: 212 431 2588
Fax: 212 431 2639

Steve Stoute
Stiggedy Entertainment
Interscope Records
825 Eighth Ave.
New York, NY 10019
Tel: 212 445 3693
Fax: 212 445 3400

Troy Patterson
Third Street Music Group USA
210 The Plaza, Suite 10
Teaneck, NJ 07666
Tel: 201 833 4046
Fax: 201 833 4599

Tony Davis
T-Luv Management
3018 Gary Dr.
St. Louis, MO 63121
Tel: 314 385 1848
Fax: 314 383 2393

Herb Trawick
The Trawick Group
4640 Dunas Ln.
Tarzana, CA 91356
Tel: 818 342 1844
Fax: 818 342 8951

Doug Brown
Wright Entertainment Group
4717 Posada Dr.
Orlando, FL 32839
Tel: 407 826 9100
Fax: 407 826 9107

Pop/Urban

Steven Rosen
Pop/Urban
All Ears Management
4007 West Magnolia Blvd.
Burbank, CA 91505
Tel: 818 843 2628
Fax: 818 843 4480

Steven Kurt
Pop/Urban
Marquee Management
274 Madison Ave.
New York, NY 10016
Tel: 212 889 0420
Fax: 212 889 0279

Johnny Wright
Pop/Urban
Wright Entertainment Group USA
4717 Posada Dr.
Orlando, FL 32839
Tel: 407 826 9100
Fax: 407 826 9107

Rock/Urban

Kevin Law
Uncommon Management NY
200 West 57th St., Suite 401
New York, NY 10019
Tel: 212 586 0222

Pop/Rock/Urban/MoR/Country

Andrew Slater
Andrew Slater Management
9200 Sunset Blvd.
Las Angeles, CA 90069
Tel: 310 550 5240
Fax: 310 550 5241

Carlos Santana
Santana Management USA
P.O. Box 10348
San Rafael, CA 94912
Tel: 415 458 8130
Fax: 415 458 8145

Entertainment Attorneys

Never sign a contract without consulting an attorney. This list will
help you start your search process
when you need a lawyer.

AAA Attorney Referral Service Inc.
800 733 6337

Abdo and Abdo P.A.
612 333 1526

Abrams, Jo Ann Attorney At Law
561 791 1989

Alfred Kim Guggenheim, Esq.
310 441 8000

Anthony B. Timpano II
860 448 6181

Avacom
305 667 7477

Barron, Newburger and Associates P.C.
512 476 9103

Baxtor, Charles T., Attorney
502 588 2004

Berger, Kahn
310 821 9000

Berliner, Corcoran and Rowe
301 570 1761

Blackman, A. Lee, Attorney at Law
818 981 4311

Bloom, Dekon and Hergott
310 859 6800

Boston Entertainment Law Group
617 965 4570

Brauer, Andrea, Attorney at Law
213 661 2440

Brooks and Associates P.C.
516 338 0533

Burke and Castle P.C.
303 299 1800

California Lawyers For The Arts
415 775 7200

Carp, Sexauer and Carb
314 863 4300

Charne, James I., Attorney at Law
310 458 9345

Chernau, Chaffin, and Burnsed PLLC
615 244 5480

Chopnick, Max
212 696 1050

Cohon and Gardner, P.C.
310 277 4701

Craig Benson Law Office
615 320 0660

David M. Adler and Associates P.C.
312 255 0199

Degensheim, I Attorney at Law
415 241 7300

Diamond and Wilson
310 820 7808

Dillard and Noel
312 606 0100

Dodson, Parker and Behm
615 254 2291

Donnelly Bob, Attorney at Law
212 683 8775

Edelstein, Laird and Sobel LLP
310 274 6184

Elliot Cahn, Esq.
510 652 1615

EMB Financial Group Inc.
310 662 0785

Entertainment Law and Finance
917 256 2115

Ervin, Cohen, Jessup
310 273 6333

Eversley
212 678 7064

Farano Green
416 961 2344

Fischbach, Medows and Perlstein
310 556 1956

Fisher, Wayland and Copper
202 659 3494

Franklin Douglas
212 865 5249

Garvey, Schubert and Barer
206 464 3939

Gibson, Dunn, Crutcher
213 229 7000

Glassman and Browning Inc.
310 278 5100

Goldman and Kagon
310 552 1707

Goodman and Goodman
416 979 2211

Gowling, Strathy and Henderson
416 862 7525

Graves, Dougherty, Heaton and Moody
512 480 5600

Greenberg Traurig
404 237 7700

Greenstein Law Office
818 225 8917

Grubman, Indursky and Schindler
212 554 0400

Hall, Dickeler, Kent, Goldstein and
   Wood LLP
310 203 8410

Hayes and Company, CPAS
612 349 9290

Herzog, Gary, Attorney at Law
213 876 5920

Hudson and Associates, P.C.
404 897 5252

Ira C. Selkowitz, Attorney at Law
303 692 0077

J. Scott "Skip" Rudsenske
615 228 6005

Jackson and Walker
214 953 5805

Janklow, Newborn and Ashley
212 421 1700

Johnson and Rishwain, LLP
310 826 2410

Joseph C. Fraulob, Attorney at Law
916 492 7625

Ken Hamilton, Attorney at Law
512 474 1554

Kenneth L. Kunkle Attorney
612 414 3113

Kettle III
973 491 3942

Kopsick, Steven, Esq.
212 477 5654

Law Office of Cynthia M. Cleves
606 331 2050

Law Office of Joseph R. Cruse
562 901 4826

Law Office of Miriam Stern
212 794 1289

Leonard, James M.
310 821 9000

Levine and Miller
310 278 9750

Lisa A. Cervantes, Attorney at Law
619 339 8685

Luneau, John P.
215 248 3898

M. Becker Esq.
212 759 8193

Manier, Herod, Hollabaugh and Smith
615 244 0030

Mark A. Infante-Attorney at Law
973 325 3808

Martin, Serge G., Law Office
305 443 2910

Leibowitz
212 275 2950

McGarry, Charles Law Office
214 748 0800

McMillan Binch
416 865 7111

Michael C. Lasser, Esq.
212 459 1919

Michael R. Diliberto
310 557 1511

Mirecki Inc.
949 854 6464

Mitchell, Silberberg and Knupp
310 312 2000

Moore, Steven, Walker and Rhoads
615 244 7300

Morris and Florey LLP
512 479 8600

Myman, Abell, Fineman and Greenspan
310 820 7717

Nelson, Guggenheim, Felker and Levine LLP
310 441 8000

O'Connel and Aronowitz
518 462 5601

Ober, Kaler, Grimes and Shriver
410 347 7388

Opatrny, Esq.
518 537 5580

Orlando Records, LLC
407 673 0599

Palmer and Dodge
617 573 0100

Paul B. Ungar, Esq.
732 906 2061

Penton, Ronnie
504 732 5651

Peter Thall, Attorney at Law
212 245 6221

Phillips, Esq.
310 312 4111

Pierce and Gorman
310 274 9191

Polk and Berke
310 571 2808

Pryor, Cashman, Sherman and Flynn
212 326 0127

Redlich, Attorney at Law
310 453 8017

Resources and Counseling For The Arts
612 292 3206

Rishwain
213 937 0139

Rohde and Victoroff
310 277 1482

Rosenblum, Stewart
631 367 8544

Ross, Jay B. and Associates P.C.
312 633 9000

Rubin, Bailin, Ortoli, Mayer and Baker
212 935 0900

Russell E. Rains
512 479 0744

Sanderson, Attorney
416 971 6616

Schiff and Shelton
714 438 2211

Schneider, Goldberg, Rohatiner and Yuen
310 274 8201

Sherrill and Weir Inc.
615 269 6755

Shukat, Hafer and Weber
212 245 4580

Singer, Netter & Dowd
212 486 8600

Skiena, Alan
212 664 1131

Solomon & Associates
615 726 0400

Staehely, Jr., Al, Attorney
713 528 6946

Steptoe and Johnson
202 429 8089

Stryker, Tams and Dill LLP
973 491 9500

Texas Accountants and Lawyers For The Arts
713 526 4876

Tormey, John J. III.
212 410 4142

Trock, Kevin C., Esq.
312 661 2100

Varty and Company
604 684 5356

Volunteer Lawyers For The Arts
212 319 2787

Weinstein and Hart
310 274 7157

Wolf, Greenfield and Sacks
617 720 3500

Wyatt, Tarrant, Combs, and Milom
615 255 6161

Ziffren, Brittenham and Branca
310 552 3388

Zumwalt, Almon, Hayes
615 256 7200

Online Hip-Hop
The best hop-hop sites on the Net.

13 Floor Entertainment
13thfloorent.com
Featured talented hip hop artists, such as Gener'al. Info, audio, merchandise, and more.

1 Redline Productions
redlineproductions.com
A non-profit indie label dedicated to helping artists achieve their desired objectives, and musical goals.

Brick Records
brickrecords.com
Official Website for Brick Records.

Celestial Productions
celestialproductions.com
Artists looking for hot underground hip-hop beats, check us out. We also develop web sites, so check us out.

DjSwindle
djswindle.com
High-End Hip-Hop. This website is devoted to hip-hop music and the artists on the Swindle Entertainment record label. Rappers such as Logic, Rok One and more. Also home to the 'Virtual Turntable'. Come on over and play with some records!

Dollar Bill Records
dollarbillrecords.ca
Independent record label. Specializes in hip-hop remixes & party records; also new artists. Download free music.

Funk Squad Entertainment

funksquadent.com

An independent music label supporting the production of hip hop/ rap and R&B

Goldeneyes Entertainment

goldeneyesonline.com

The online home for Goldeneyes Entertainment. Listen to the pioneering Ragga Hop & Hip Blues sounds coming out of One Kool Studio.

HandSolo Records

handsolorecords.com

Home to the best in Canadian hip hop. Seriously skilled artists, seriously tight label.

Indie Pennant

www.indiepennant.com

Indie Label for some of the illest indie artists.

Kamikaze Records

kamikazerecords.com

San Francisco Bay Area-based record label specializing in hip-hop, pop, R&B, dance, and alternative music. Independent record label creates music related to all the masses, and also helps and develops artists that strive to break into the mainstream music scene.

Kismana Music

www.kismana.com.au

Australian Independent Music. CDs, Audio tapes, MP3 samples of Independent Australian Artists available. Songwriting tips and resources. Subscribe to K.I.S., an Ezine for keen independent songwriters.

Legal Damage Productions

www.legaldamage.com

Independent underground label. Introducing DJ Wryck, mp3s, downloads, raplinx, FREE breakbeats & hip-hop news.

Lindy-Records

lindyrecords.addr.com

Source for independent music, offering a wide variety of online tool to help independent musicians promote and sell their material.

Low Life Records

lowliferecords.co.uk

The U.K.'s number one hip-hop label

OPE Entertainment

angelfire.com/on/ope

Official label website. "Beats for da streets." Brooklyn NYC's HARDEST rap label.

Plan Z Media

www.planznow.com

An independent label dedicated to the production and distribution of music and cinema.

Premiere Records

tinpan.fortunecity.com/foottap/1195

Premiere Records are dedicated to promoting the online musician. Listen to our showcase artists and join our email list for the latest in promotion and industry news.

Rap Junkie Records

rapjunkierecords.com

Rap Junkie Records—Los Angeles-based independent rap label, featuring B. Down and the Congriz Crew.

Supa Cindy

www.supacindyonline.com

Get the latest gossip, news, and entertainment from the multi-cultural mami herself, Supa Cindy: The skirt with the dirt.

Stray Records

www.strayrecords.com

Well-known and successful hip-hop record label, featuring talented artists such as Azeem.

Thermite Records

thermiterecords.com

Home of Mello-D & the Rados, the hottest touring live hip-hop band in the U.S.! Check out tour dates, sound bites, pics, reviews and much more.

Treal Records

www.trealrecords.com

The crunkest underground label out of Miami.

Industry Contracts

Here are some sample industry agreements. Read them over to get familiar with the language. And remember, never sign a contract without having an attorney advise you first.

Production Agreement

INDEPENDENT PRODUCTION AGREEMENT

This agreement is made between _____. (Producer) and _____(Artist). In Consideration of the mutual promises contained herein, the parties agree as follows:

Scope and Purpose Producer hereby engages Artist's exclusive personal services as recording artist for the immediate purpose of producing and exploiting a record containing not less than Forty-Five (45) minutes of playing time (Master).

As a further purpose, Producer and Artist agree to seek a recording contract with a nationally distributed record company (Recording Contract) providing for minimum combined artist-producer royalty of not less than Twelve percent (12%) of the retail-selling price of all records embodying Master.

Producer Duties Producer agrees to provide production services as an independent producer and the necessary studio facilities to Artist. Producer shall manage, supervise, organize all aspects pertaining to the creation and production of Master including, without limitation, the selection, and arrangement and mixing of musical composition(s) included in Master.

Artist Duties Artist shall deliver to Producer a technically satisfactory Master as determined by Producer. Artist shall use good faith and best efforts in providing recording services to ensure the high quality performance that induced Producer to engage Artist. Artist further agrees to comply with all reasonable rules, regulations, instructions, requests, or other requirement as determined by Producer in connection with the production of Master.

Term The term of this Agreement shall begin on the date this Agreement is signed (Effective Date) and shall continue for Twelve (12) months after delivery of the first Master (Initial Period). Artist hereby grants the Producer Four (4) option(s) to extend the term upon the same conditions and duration of the Initial Period.

Compensation Artist shall pay Producer a production fee $_____ per Master (Track), payable at the commencement of the (Recording Contract). Artist shall request and authorize payment of Royalty directly to Producer and such payment shall be considered an advance to Artist only.

If Producer or Artist obtains a recording and distribution contract (Recording Contract) for the commercial exploitation of a Master produced under this Agreement, Producer shall be entitled to a Royalty of Three percent (3%) of the suggested retail list price (SLRP) on all records embodying the Master sold in the U.S. less customary adjustments for packaging, promotional goods, and foreign market sales.

Recording Costs All recording costs incurred by Producer in connection with Artist's service under this contract The Artist shall be fully responsible for all recording cost in connection with the production of Master and all such costs shall be considered an Advance and set off against Artist's Royalties.

Grant of Rights Beginning on the date when a Master Recording is delivered to Producer, Producer shall be the exclusive owner of rights to all Master Recordings for the period of time of 18 months (one year six months) the "Ownership Period".

During Ownership Period, Artist grants to Producer all right, title and interest in the sound recording copyright (as provided under the U.S. Copyright Act of 1976 and international copyright treaties) to the Master Recording

* The exclusive right to manufacture copies of all or any portion of the Master Recordings;
* The exclusive right to import, export, sell, transfer, release, license, publicly perform, rent, and otherwise exploit or dispose of the Master Recording; and
* The exclusive rights to edit adapt or conform the Master Recordings to technological or commercial requirements in various formats now known or later developed.

Territory The rights granted to Producer are limited to the world (the "Territory")

Exclusivity Artist shall only render recording services for the Producer during this Agreement and shall not render such services to any other individual or entity for _____ months after the termination of this Agreement, without the written permission of the Producer.

Breach Artist hereby acknowledges that Artist's recording services provided in connection with this Agreement are unique and extraordinary and that Producer shall be entitled to both legal and equitable remedies, including injunctive relief, in the event of a threatened or actual breach.

Right to Use Artist' Name and Likeness Producer shall have the right to reproduce or distribute in any medium, Artist's names, portraits, pictures and likeness for purposes of advertising, promotion or trade in connection with Artist or the exploitation of the Master Recordings. Artist shall be available from time to time appear for photography, video performance or the like, under the reasonable direction of Producer, Artist shall not be entitled to any compensation for such services.

Side-Artist Recording During the Term, Artist may perform as part of another artist' recording project (a "side-artist" performance) provided that. (a) the side-artist recording does not interfere with obligations under this Agreement and (b) the following credit is included on the side-artist recording." _____ Appears courtesy _____ productions.

Subsequent Recording of Compositions Artist represents and warrants that Artist shall not record any composition contained on a Master Recording for a period of _____ months (_____) years from the date of delivery of Master Recording to Producer.

Artist Warranties. Artist warrants to Producer that Artist has the power and authority to enter into this Agreement and that Artist's use of any musical composition or arrangement will not infringe on the rights of orders.

Controlled Composition License Artist grants to Producer an irrevocable worldwide license to reproduce all compositions wholly or party written, owned or controlled by Artist (the "Controlled Composition").

Termination Producer or Artist may terminate this Agreement within Thirty 30) days of the expiration of the Term or any Option Period. Any termination of this Agreement shall not terminate the underlying license and copyrights granted to Producer by Artist.

Governing Law & Entire Agreement This agreement shall be governed by and interpreted in accordance with the laws of the State of _____. This Agreement expresses the complete understanding of the parties with respect to the subject matter and supersedes all proposals, agreements, representations and understandings.

Notices required under this agreement can be sent to the parties at the address provided below.
IN WITNESS WHEREOF, THE PARTIES SIGN AND SEAL THIS AGREEMENT:

_____

Artist Name

_____

Address

_____

_____

S.S.N.

_____

Producer Name

Work-for-Hire Agreement

WHEREAS,_____

_____

(Hereinafter referred as "Employee") has and/or will at the request of

_____(Employer)

and upon Employer's special order and commission rendered services as

_____

_____and

WHEREAS, Employee and Employer agree that the said services of the employee be considered, as works made for hire as contemplated and defined in Section 101 of the United States Copyright act;

NOW THEREFORE, in consideration of the sum of_____($_____)

Dollars, and other good and valuable consideration, receipt of which is hereby acknowledged, Employee does hereby acknowledge such employment and that under the terms of such employment performances embodied in any and all masters, records and other media formats and all rights appertaining thereto (including, without limitation, all computer generated custom sounds and control programs therefore) are entirely the property of the Employer, its successors and assigns, absolutely and forever, for any and all copyright terms and all extension and renewal terms of copyright whether now or hereafter created throughout the world, and for all uses and purposes whatsoever and free from the payment of any royalty or compensation whatsoever. **The fee provided is as negotiated by and between the Producer and the Employee. If you have any questions concerning the processing and payment of this Agreement, please contact the Producer.**

IN WITNESS WHEREOF, the parties have hereunto set their hands and seals

the_____ day of_____,_____

Name:_____ _____
                                          Home Phone Number
Signature:_____ _____
                                          Business Phone Number
Address:_____

_____

_____
                Producer
SS#:_____

_____
                Signature
Hours from:_____ to_____

                    Title Of Track (s):

1)_____   Time:_____

2)_____   Time:_____

3)_____   Time:_____

4)_____   Time:_____

Project Name:_____

Recording Location(s):_____

PROCESSING OF PAYMENT WILL BE RENDERED WITHIN 30 DAYS OF SUBMISSION

Please keep a copy of this Agreement for your records<B>

Sub-Publishing Agreement
SUB-PUBLISHING AGREEMENT

AGREEMENT made this _____ day of _____, 200_, by and between _____ (hereinafter called the "Owner"), and _____ (hereinafter called the "sub-publisher").

WHEREAS, the sub-publisher is desirous of obtaining certain rights in the musical composition (hereinafter called the "Composition"), now entitled:

SONG TITLE

a song by _____, for the term herein set forth, and for the territory of:

EXTENT OF LICENSING TERRITORY
only, (herein called the "Territory").

NOW THEREFORE, in consideration of the sum of One Dollar and other good and valuable considerations, each to the other in hand paid, receipt of which is

hereby acknowledged, it is hereby agreed as follows:

1. The Owner hereby grants to the Sub-Publisher, for the licensed territory

only, and for a term equal to the balance of the term of the first United States published copyright of the Composition, all rights existing under the copyrights of the Song for the Territory, including, but not limited, the words and music thereof, the right to print, publish, and vend the Composition in the licensed Territory, and all performing rights, and synchronization rights and mechanical rights of the Composition in the licensed Territory and all claims and demands relating thereto; except only as limited in this Agreement.

2. The foregoing assignment is made subject to the following terms and conditions:

(a) The Owner reserves all rights in and to all copyrights of the Composition and all the rights of any and every nature thereunder existing, for all the countries of the world outside the licensed Territory.

(b) The Owner reserves the exclusive right to license world-wide uses of the title of the Composition as a title for Motion Pictures.

(c) The grant of performing rights is subject to the rights of _____. The Sub-Publisher shall cause the performing and broadcast rights of the Song to be registered with the performing rights societies in the licensed Territory so as to provide that the entire publisher's share of performing fees and broadcasting fees shall be credited and paid to the Owner. The Sub-Publisher shall account to the Owner with respect thereto in accordance with Paragraph " 3 (b) (iii)".

(d) The Sub-Publisher shall have the right to issue non-exclusive world-wide licenses for the synchronization of the Composition with sound motion pictures. If such motion pictures are produced and originate in the

Territory. The Owner reserves unto itself the exclusive right to grant licenses for the entire world for the synchronization of the Composition with sound motion pictures, if such sound motion pictures are produced and originate outside of the Territory, and the Sub-publisher shall not be entitled to share in any world-wide fees received by Owner in respect of any such world-wide licenses.

3. The Sub-Publisher agrees to pay the Owner the following royalties in respect of the Composition.

(a) An amount equal to TEN (10%) percent of the marked retail selling price of each and every copy of whatsoever kind and nature of the Composition, sold and paid for under the authority of this Agreement.

(b) An amount equal to FIFTY (50%) PERCENT of all moneys received by the Second Party for

(i) mechanical licenses issued by Sub-Publisher in respect of the Composition,

(ii) synchronization licenses issued by it in respect of sound motion pictures produced and originated in the Territory, and

(iii) performing fees and broadcasting fees received by Sub-Publisher in respect of public performances for profit of the Territory.

4. The Sub-Publisher may reprint the Song in any folio, and in such event, the Sub-Publisher shall pay the Owner, a royalty of that proportion of TEN (10%) PERCENT of the net wholesale selling price of such folios sold and paid for as the Composition shall bear to all of the musical compositions contained in such folios.

5. The Sub-Publisher shall have the right to arrange and adapt the Composition, and to translate the lyrics of the Composition into languages of the Territory, or have a new title and lyrics written therefore, and said arrangements, adaptations, translations and new title and lyrics shall be the property of the Owner, subject to the rights of the Sub-Publisher hereunder.

6. The Sub-Publisher shall keep true and accurate books of account, which shall at all times be open to inspection during regular business hours by the Owner. The Sub-Publisher shall prepare and forward to the Owner a detailed and itemized statement semi-annually in each year, in or about 45 days after the end of each calendar half-year, for said calendar half-year, and each statement shall be accompanied by a remittance in the currencies of the Territory for all amounts to be due thereunder less taxes, if any. Said accounting and payment, in the absence of written objection thereto by the Owner within ONE YEAR from the receipt thereof, shall constitute an account stated as to all royalties due for the period encompassed by such statement and/or payment.

7. The Sub-Publisher agrees that on each copy of the Composition published by the Sub-Publisher, there shall be printed the notice of copyright prescribed by the Owner, together with a notification of the assignment of the rights for the Territory.

8. The Sub-Publisher agrees to deliver to the Owner, without any charge, a copy of all editions of the Composition printed by it pursuant to the authority of this Agreement.

9. The Sub-Publisher may assign any of its rights hereunder to any other publishers for any countries of the Territory, provided that the Sub-Publisher shall remain primarily liable for the payment of royalties hereunder.

10. With respect to the Territory, the Owner Warrants that the Composition is and shall be new and original, that it does not and shall not infringe any other copyrighted work, and that the Owner has the full right and power to enter into this Agreement and grant the rights herein granted by it. The Owner shall hold the Sub-Publisher, its successors, assigns, licensees and nominees free and harmless from any and all claims, costs, and damages arising from any breach of the aforementioned warranties.

11. The Owner hereby appoints the Sub-Publisher and its assigns, its agent and attorney-in-fact, to institute in the name of the Owner, as copyright owner of the Composition, any suit, action or proceeding in the Territory, which the Sub-Publisher or its assigns shall in its discretion deem necessary for the protection of rights herein assigned to it, and the Sub-Publisher hereby agrees to indemnify and hold harmless the Owner of and from any and all obligation to pay any costs, expenses or disbursements with respect to any such suit, action or proceeding, This paragraph shall in no way relieve the Owner from any responsibility to the Sub-Publisher with respect to any breaches by the Owner of the any of the terms of this Agreement.

12. **ALL ROYALTIES PAYABLE UNDER THIS AGREEMENT SHALL BE BASED ON INCOME RECEIVED AT THE SOURCE.**

13. This Agreement shall be binding upon and shall inure to the benefits of the parties hereto and their respective successors and assigns.

14. This Agreement shall be construed in accordance with and governed by the

laws of the State of _____. Should any portion of this Agreement be found to be invalid or unenforceable, it shall not affect the balance of this Agreement.

15. Sub-Publisher promises to make all of its contracts, correspondences, bills, invoices, books and files concerning the Composition available to representatives of Owner upon one week's notice.

16. Sub-Publisher agrees to pay Owner at the time Sub-Publisher and Owner have both signed and executed this Agreement an advance of _____.

IN WITNESS WHEREOF, the parties have caused this Agreement to be signed by their duly authorized officers the day and year above set forth.

OWNER_____

By: _____
Address
City, State, Zip

SUB-PUBLISHER_____

By: _____
Address
City, State, Zip

Epilogue

To further your education in the music business, check us out at:

www.gottagetsigned.com

The End,
Peace Out

What Others Are Saying About This Book

"Welcome to your reality check. Read this book and step up your game."

—DJ Laz "The Pimp with the Limp"
radio personality, DJ, producer, and artist

"Remarkably observant view of hip hop's innards. This book is a smart raw study of the real music business. Read and learn."

—"Dr Paul" Hamilton,
reggae producer/musician

"REAL, RAW, DESRCRIPTIVE, AND MOST OF ALL, INTELLIGENT. This account of one man's journey in the entertainment business allows any newcomer to realize first that this business is sometimes not what it's cut out to be. It's GANGSTA and RUTHLESS! Learn from a PRO what it takes to work hard and value the roller-coaster life one must endure to be successful."

—Jammin' Johnny Caride, promotions director and marketing
Spanish Broadcasting Systems Inc.

"This is the first music biz book that uses street smarts and common sense to educate new jax and veterans in the game. To all the wannabe's trying to make it big in the game, learn from the author's personal journey to the championship. If you're already in the game, go sit on the bench and read this book. Stay focused and read wisely. Good luck!"

—Afrika (Nathaniel Hall),
Jungle Brothers

"If only this informative hip-hop manual would have come out years ago, we wouldn't have all the clueless, confused, broke, and ego-driven one-hit wonders, wannabe rappers, and industry power movers in this game today!"

—Supa Cindy,
hip-hop radio personality/Gossip Diva

"This book shows a hungry artist/producer how to skip all the hotdog stands in the industry and get to the real meal."

—J. Bishop, actor/host
The Roof on Mun2

"As an artist, songwriter, and producer I think this book is right-on-time for those who are entering the music business. It outlines how to get into the business, as well as how to be business savvy. It speaks to you in a down to earth language; this can help change the way the game is played."

—Walter "Clyde" Orange Commodores, Inc
Grammy award-winning producer/artist

"The book is a must have, it gives an honest insight to the game of hip hop. The resources and extras alone will help you become a better player."

—Chris Hudspeth, director
Connecticut School of Broadcasting
Davie Campus

"The book is very informative for someone that is try'n 2 get into the entertainment business; this book is very much worth the look."

—DJ Suicide,
TV/radio personality